San Francisco
RUNNING
Guide

CITY
RUNNING GUIDE
SERIES

BOB COOPER

Human Kinetics

Library of Congress Cataloging-in-Publication Data

Cooper, Bob, 1954-
   San Francisco running guide / Bob Cooper.
      p.   cm. -- (City running guide series)
   ISBN 0-88011-703-6
   1. Running--California--San Francisco Bay Area--Guidebooks.
   2. San Francisco Bay Area (Calif.)--Guidebooks. I. Title. II. Series
   GV1061.22.C2C66   1998
   796.42′5′0979461--dc21

                                                      97-47673
ISBN: 0-88011-703-6   CIP

Acquisitions Editor: Martin Barnard; **Developmental Editor:** Julie Rhoda; **Assistant Editor:** Sandra Merz Bott; **Editorial Assistant:** Laura T. Seversen; **Copyeditor:** Cynthia Hastings; **Proofreader:** Kathy Bennett; **Graphic Designer:** Stuart Cartwright; **Graphic Artist:** Kimberly Maxey; **Photo Managers:** Boyd LaFoon and Tom Roberts; **Cover Designer:** Jack Davis; **Photographer (cover):** Ken Lee (photo taken on Golden Gate Bridge during 1989 San Francisco Marathon); **Photographer (interior):** Ken Lee; **Illustrators:** Jennifer Delmotte, Kimberly Maxey, and Kimberly Michael; **Printer:** Versa Press

Printed in the United States of America   10 9 8 7 6 5 4 3 2

Human Kinetics
Web site: http://www.humankinetics.com/

United States: Human Kinetics, P.O. Box 5076, Champaign, IL 61825-5076
1-800-747-4457
e-mail: humank@hkusa.com

Canada: Human Kinetics, Box 24040, Windsor, ON N8Y 4Y9
1-800-465-7301 (in Canada only)
e-mail: humank@hkcanada.com

Europe: Human Kinetics, P.O. Box IW14, Leeds LS16 6TR, United Kingdom
(44) 1132 781708
e-mail: humank@hkeurope.com

Australia: Human Kinetics, 57A Price Avenue, Lower Mitcham, South Australia 5062
(088) 277 1555
e-mail: humank@hkaustralia.com

New Zealand: Human Kinetics, P.O. Box 105-231, Auckland 1
(09) 523 3462
e-mail: humank@hknewz.com

CONTENTS

INTRODUCTION

I don't know of any other city where ... you're never out of sight of the wild hills. Nature is very close here.

—Gary Snyder, Pulitzer Prize-winning poet

Snyder is describing San Francisco, where countless runners have left their hearts on the Hayes Street hill at the Bay to Breakers race and countless more have fallen hard for those wild hills of the Bay Area. You can find runners on any postcard weekend (which is almost every weekend) tickling the trails and racing the roads.

This book is an attempt to present the crème de la crème. In the best place to run and race in America, if not the world, where are the best running trails, paths, and roads, and which are the best races?

Before I started my research by plotting and running each of these routes, a dream job if there ever was one, I frankly didn't expect to learn much. I already knew that the Bay Area boasted parklands accounting for nearly a million of the Bay Area's 4.5 million acres. I had run and raced in the Bay Area for 21 years—six years in the South Bay, seven in San Francisco, and the last nine in the North Bay. But I did get an education. The number of spectacular running oases throughout the Bay Area was a shock, making it difficult to decide which runs and races to include.

You may wonder why I didn't pick your favorite training route. Well, here are the factors I considered while trimming the field.

• Is it an area with an extensive network of runner-friendly trails or bike paths? I usually include one route in each area, and sometimes a shorter or longer alternate route. This gives you an introduction to the area. On subsequent outings you can explore other trails depending on the distance and terrain that you prefer. Most parks provide free trail maps (this book includes phone numbers) to let you customize later runs.

• Is it easy to abbreviate or extend the route? Some days you just want to go shorter—or longer—because of the weather or your energy level. I've included many out-and-back routes, which let you turn back at any time, and most routes connect to other trails that enable you to go farther. In some instances, a main route and an alternate route are described and shown on the map.

• Are there many street crossings? Few things are more annoying than waiting for red lights, sucking up auto exhaust, and worrying about reckless or abusive drivers. You won't be near cars on most of these routes.

• Is the trip to the starting point enjoyable? The drive to some of these routes is as scenic as the running that follows.

• Is the trip to the start too darn long? All but a handful of these courses are within 30 minutes of San Francisco or San Jose, and only one run (Point Reyes) and one race (the Big Sur Marathon) are more than an hour's drive from both cities—but they are worth the drive!

• Is parking a hassle? Parking is free for every route except Lake Merritt ($2 on weekends only) and Coyote Creek (a $3 self-service fee that is seldom enforced).

The final mix of courses is full of variety. Variety also describes the Bay Area's unusual climate. Temperatures can vary by 30 degrees on afternoons when it is foggy on the coast and hot 30 miles inland. Here are the typical conditions within the Bay Area:

Summer: Cool and foggy (50s and 60s) near the coast, and warm (60s to 90s) inland.

Autumn: Cool mornings (50s and 60s) and warmer afternoons (60s to 80s) everywhere.

Winter: Highs in the 50s and 60s, lows in the 30s and 40s, with the most rain in the North Bay and the least in the South Bay.

Spring: Highs in the 60s to 80s, with mornings in the 50s. Afternoons are usually windy.

Trail courses are periodically closed during warm and windy periods in the summer due to fire danger, so call the park before heading out. Phone numbers of parks are included.

Most of the courses are on wide, well-traveled paths with few daytime hazards, but here are a few words of caution:

Poison oak: It is most noticeable in the fall when the three-pointed leaves turn orange-red, but you can get the itch any time of year. To avoid this burning rash, wash the exposed area in cold water and apply Tecnu cleanser (the choice of most parklands workers, available over-the-counter at most drug stores) immediately after possible exposure.

Ticks: On narrow trails where your calves brush against tall grasses, these tiny critters are blood-sucking hitchhikers. Inspect your body, especially your lower legs, after such runs. If you find one embedded in your skin, remove the whole body with tweezers and wash and bandage the area.

Rattlesnakes: Encounters are usually in rocky areas in the summer, but are very rare. Back away slowly.

Mountain lions: As with rattlers, you'll probably never see one. If you do encounter a mountain lion, stop running, face the lion, and raise your arms to make yourself "large." Forget about outrunning it, even if you're Michael Johnson.

Bad guys and bad drivers: These are the truly threatening creatures, especially for women. On streets, run against traffic and wear reflective material after dark. On routes where there's a phone, carry change. If possible, tell someone when and where you're running, or run with someone. Consider carrying pepper spray, which requires no permit in California. Don't wear headsets or jewelry.

The greatest peril for runners, especially those over age 40, is running or racing in the absence of physical readiness or in the presence of undetected heart disease. Get an OK from a doctor if you aren't already exercising vigorously or if you haven't seen one in awhile, then build your mileage slowly. Even if you are in good shape, take walking breaks or shorten a route if your body demands it. At the least, it could save you from the doldrums on your next run. At most, it could save your life.

Before heading to any of these routes, call TravInfo, 510-817-1717 (817-1717 within the Bay Area). TravInfo provides up-to-the-minute reports on road conditions and tie-ups that could affect your trip; timetable information for all of the Bay Area's 25 transit systems (buses, light-rail, rail, and ferries); and information on bicycle accessibility.

Within each course description you will find:

1. an introduction explaining why this is somewhere you'll want to run;
2. access information that tells you how to get to the starting point;
3. course information that describes every turn on the run (tear the page out and take it with you); and
4. "Foot Notes" that provide additional information to help you enjoy the run. Some routes also include sidebar stories and tips.

The map that accompanies each route description usually shows the roads that lead you to your parking spot, other major roads and trails in the area, and roads and trails you will follow on the running route.

Chapters are grouped by Bay Area sections: San Francisco, North Bay (Marin County), East Bay (Alameda and Contra Costa Counties) and South Bay (San Mateo and Santa Clara Counties). Each chapter opens with a description of running in that area and an overview map to help you get oriented to the freeway system. Races described in the closing chapter are those that are well-loved, well-attended, and within easy driving distance of the Bay Area.

ICON KEY

Distance Given in miles	**8.2 MILES**
Terrain **ROAD** (asphalt, concrete) / **TRAIL** (dirt, grass) / **SAND**	
Restrooms on course	🚻
Drinking water on course	💧
Telephone on course	☎

Scenery Icons
 	
          Park 🌳   Mountain ⛰
 	
          Suburban 🏡 Beach ⛱	

SCENERY RATING ⛱⛱⛱⛱⛱	rated 1 to 5 icons
HILL RATING	rated 1 hill (flat) to 5 hills (ferocious)
Start = ● **Finish = ▲** **Turnaround = ↻**	

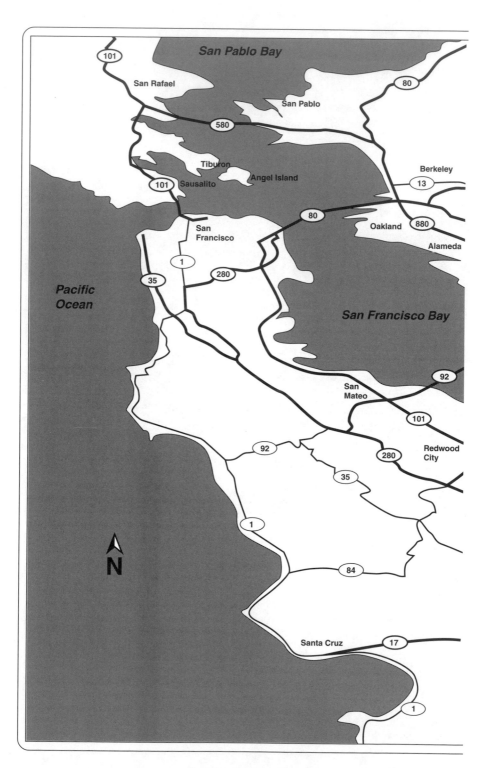

San Pablo Bay

101

San Rafael

San Pablo

80

580

Tiburon

Berkeley

Angel Island

13

101 Sausalito

80

Oakland 880

San
Francisco

Alameda

1

35

280

Pacific
Ocean

San Francisco Bay

92

San
Mateo

101

92

Redwood
City

280

35

1

N

84

Santa Cruz 17

1

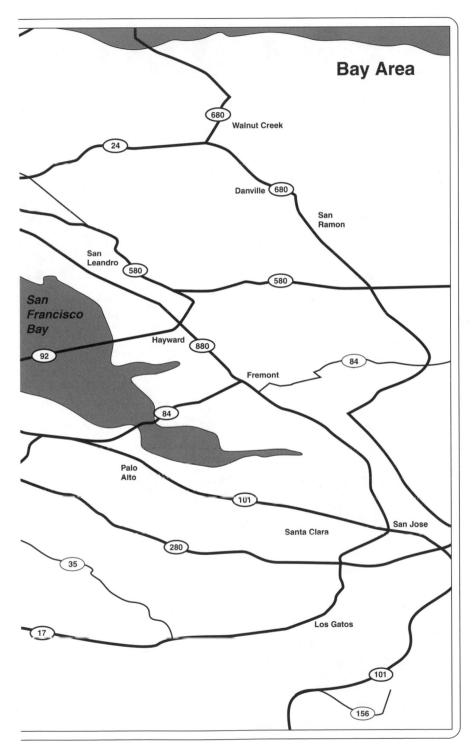

Bay Area

SAN FRANCISCO

There's no such thing as Heaven, but somewhere there is a San Francisco.

—*Mark Twain*

For a compact city (7 miles by 7 miles), San Francisco exhibits extraordinary diversity. The city comprises dozens of neighborhoods as distinct as different towns, where you can travel a few short blocks to find yourself in a place that's several degrees warmer or cooler, several hundred elevation-feet higher or lower, and radically different in the ethnic and socioeconomic makeup of its residents.

This makes the city a great place to explore between runs and a great place to race through in street events like the San Francisco Marathon and Bay to Breakers, but a lousy place to run through. In the United States, only Manhattan is more congested than San Francisco, so dodging the crazy cabbies is ill-advised. Also, the impossibly steep gradients of San Francisco's famous hills get your heart pumping too hard to be enjoyable.

Miraculously, while most of the city is a lousy place to run, a few corridors on its edges make it perhaps the best running city in the country, thanks to William Hall and the U.S. military. As the first superintendent of Golden Gate Park, Hall oversaw the dune reclamation work in the 1870s that planted the seeds for the largest urban park in America. Former military installations on the U-shaped, water-defined borders of the city have been converted into parklands, providing miles of roads, paths, and trails. Each route in this chapter is in Golden Gate Park or on former military lands.

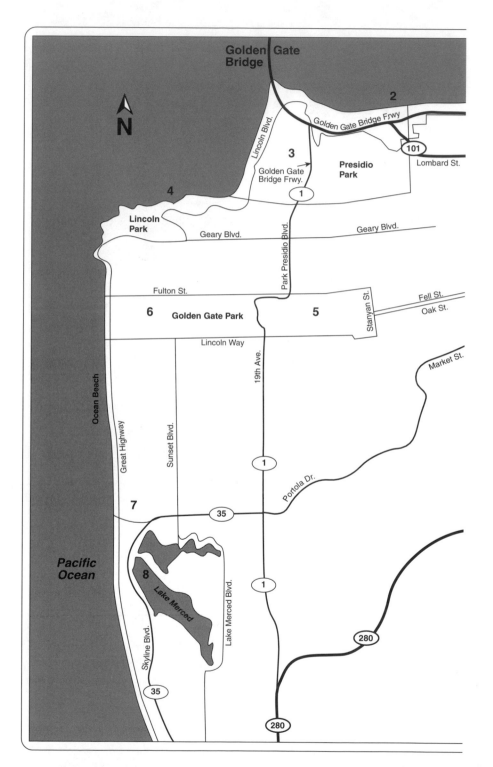

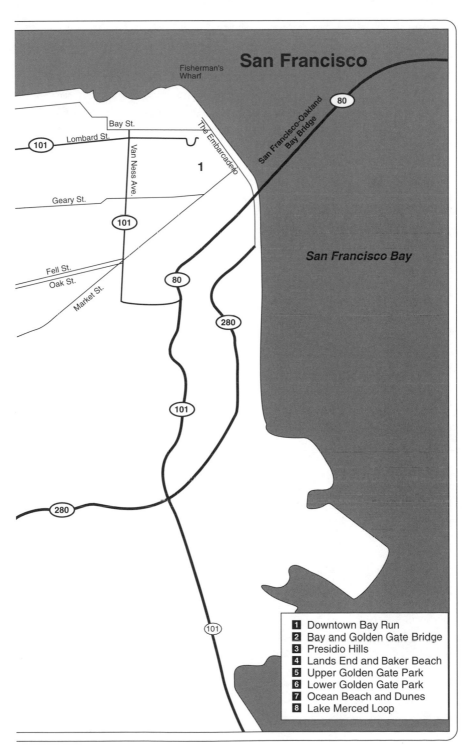

San Francisco

Fisherman's
Wharf

Bay St.

Lombard St.

Van Ness Ave.

The Embarcadero

San Francisco-Oakland
Bay Bridge

Geary St.

Fell St.

Oak St.

Market St.

San Francisco Bay

1 Downtown Bay Run
2 Bay and Golden Gate Bridge
3 Presidio Hills
4 Lands End and Baker Beach
5 Upper Golden Gate Park
6 Lower Golden Gate Park
7 Ocean Beach and Dunes
8 Lake Merced Loop

TRANSIT

San Francisco's buses, cable cars, and streetcars (which are underground only in the downtown area) are all operated by MUNI. If you're willing to transfer, you can get within a few blocks of these routes from almost anywhere in the city. For timetable info, call 415-673-MUNI. For info on public transit from outside counties to the city, call 415-817-1717.

DOWNTOWN BAY RUN

6.4 MILES	ROAD 🚻 💧 ☎	SCENERY RATING	🏖 🏖			
		HILL RATING	⛰			

Nowhere in the Bay Area will you find more runners at lunchtime than on The Embarcadero, a grand boulevard lined with palms. Most are office workers who spill onto the course from the Embarcadero YMCA and other health clubs, but this is also the San Francisco tourist's favorite course. Downtown hotels are within a short jog of the route, which is superb for fast-paced sightseeing and people watching. The course is flat and the only street crossings are at Fisherman's Wharf.

ACCESS

From downtown, take Van Ness Ave. to its end at the bay. The parking lot is rarely full, but if it is, park two blocks uphill on Bay St. Or, take the MUNI #42 bus or the Hyde St. cable car from downtown.

COURSE

Main Route. Go south along the bay—for .75 mile on a sidewalk below the Maritime Museum, on crowded Jefferson St., and the rest of the way on the bay side of The Embarcadero. Turn around at the foot of Townsend St. (near Pier 40) at the big abstract sculpture and lawn.

Alternate Route (13.2 miles). Add the Bay to Golden Gate Bridge course, starting at any point on either course.

FOOT NOTES

The first mile through Fisherman's Wharf will be an assault on your senses, from the smells of crab cocktail stands, a sourdough bakery, and landmark restaurants (Alioto's, Castagnola's, and Tarantino's) to the sights of the Wharf (19th-century ships, the Cannery, Pier 39, and a procession of touristy schlock shops). In subsequent miles, the crowds subside and you'll feel small on The Embarcadero while you pass mammoth piers, the high-rises of the financial district, and progress beneath the Bay Bridge.

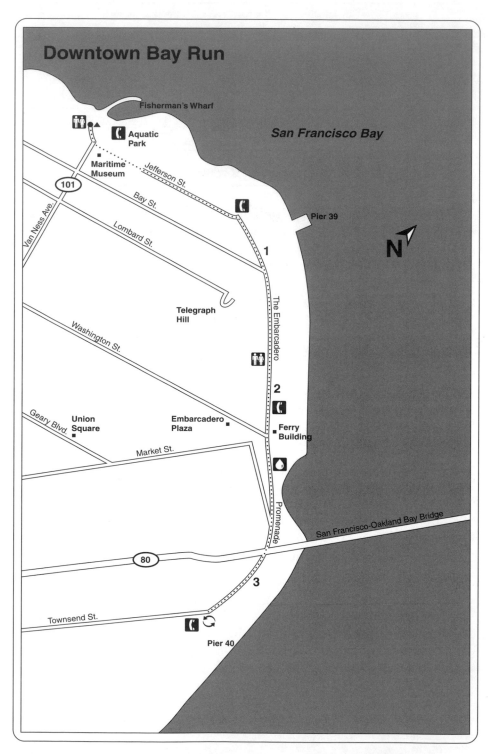

Downtown Bay Run

Fisherman's Wharf

San Francisco Bay

Aquatic Park

Maritime Museum

Jefferson St.

101

Van Ness Ave.

Bay St.

Lombard St.

Pier 39

1

N

The Embarcadero

Telegraph Hill

Washington St.

2

Geary Blvd.

Union Square

Embarcadero Plaza

Ferry Building

Market St.

Promenade

San Francisco-Oakland Bay Bridge

80

3

Townsend St.

Pier 40

BAY TO GOLDEN GATE BRIDGE

6.8 MILES	ROAD/SAND	SCENERY RATING					
	🚹🚺 💧 📞	HILL RATING					

This scenic, bay-hugging route between Aquatic Park (near Fisherman's Wharf) and the Golden Gate is peaceful as it tours remnants of past wars. Fort Mason, the Presidio, and Fort Point were all military posts dating to the 19th century, but all have been converted to peacetime uses.

ACCESS

From downtown, take Van Ness Ave. to its end at the bay. The parking lot is rarely full, but if it is, park two blocks uphill on Bay St. Or, take the MUNI #42 bus or the Hyde St. cable car from downtown.

COURSE

Main Route. Stick close to the bay, which is never more than a block away from the course. From the bottom of the parking lot, warm up by walking up the steep, 300-meter hill, and then run down the other side. Angle (R) onto Marina Blvd. for one block, then angle (R) again to the bay side of two big lawns. At the end of these lawns (Marina Green), keep straight past Yacht Harbor, slant (R) across the sunbathing lawn at St. Francis Yacht Club, then stay along the bay on a waterfront potpourri of asphalt, dirt, and beach surfaces. Turn back (you have no choice) at Fort Point, literally in the shadow of the Golden Gate Bridge.

Alternate Route (11.0 miles). At the last fishing pier before the turnaround, take the log stairs up the hill and follow To Bridge signs. Cross the 1.8-mile-long Golden Gate Bridge on the bay (R) sidewalk to the lookout area on the Marin County side. Head back.

FOOT NOTES

The main route is flat except for the first and last .5 mile; the alternate route adds a tough climb to the bridge and gradual rises on the bridge.

You won't be slowed by traffic lights on either route and instead can pay attention to the landmarks: the bridge, Marina Green (a huge kite-flying lawn so heavily used by runners that there are grooves worn into the corners), Fort Point (built in 1861), and the Fort Point sea wall, where the crashing surf may surprise you with a cold shower. Afterward, you may stroll over to Fisherman's Wharf and "warm down" with a clam chowder. For info and a map, contact Golden Gate National Recreation Area (GGNRA), 415-556-0560.

STACKED WITH TRADITION

This slice of the waterfront has a special place not only in military and civic history, but also in Bay Area running lore.

Walt Stack was the founder of the DSE Runners, the largest club in the Bay Area, and this was the first leg of his daily run for decades. He not only took the long route over the bridge, but also continued down to Sausalito and back for a hearty 17-miler, followed by a 1-mile bay swim and bike ride, of course. That training enabled Walt to finish the Western States 100-Mile and Ironman Triathlon while in his 70s. He ran his 17-mile route until he could run no more—and then he walked it. The San Franciscan was known not only for his pioneering volunteer work in running, but also for his radical politics, lovable personality, and salty jokes. He died in 1995.

This course covers most of Walt's route and also is part of several large races: the Houlihan's to Houlihan's 12K (March), San Francisco Marathon (July), Presidio 10-Mile (September), Bridge to Bridge 12K (October), and First Run 2-Mile (New Year's Eve).

TIP

High winds funnel in and out of the bay through the Golden Gate, making this stretch of bayfront one of the windier spots in North America. Windsurfers adore it, but runners must put up with fighting the head winds. Of course, you get to sail, too, in one direction.

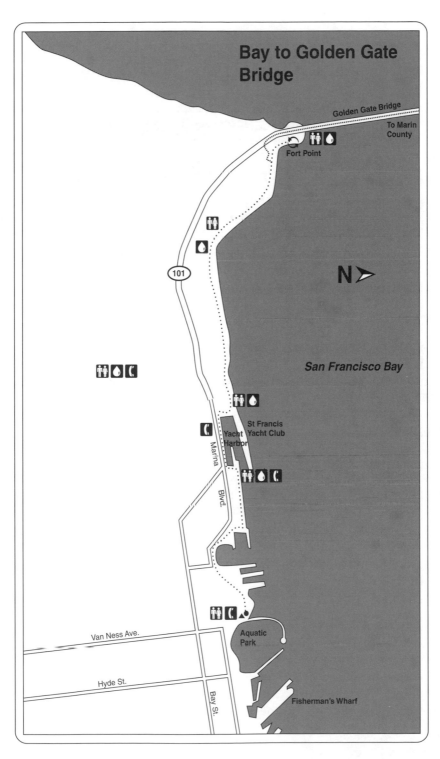

Bay to Golden Gate Bridge

Golden Gate Bridge

To Marin County

Fort Point

101

N

San Francisco Bay

St Francis Yacht Club

Yacht Harbor

Marina Blvd.

Aquatic Park

Van Ness Ave.

Hyde St.

Bay St.

Fisherman's Wharf

PRESIDIO HILLS

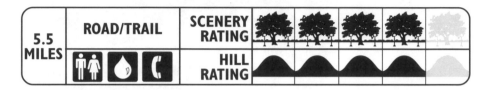

5.5 MILES	ROAD/TRAIL 👫 💧 ☎	SCENERY RATING	🌳🌳🌳🌳
		HILL RATING	⛰⛰⛰⛰

Lovers of military history and nature alike will cherish this route within the boundaries of the new, 1,480-acre Presidio National Park. Most of the route winds past tall eucalyptus and conifer trees and the tile-roofed homes of generations of Army officers. Traffic is light. On some stretches, a dirt path or shoulder parallels the road.

ACCESS

From downtown, drive north on Van Ness Ave., (L) on Lombard, (R) on Presidio Blvd., (L) on Lincoln Blvd., (L) on Montgomery (Visitor Center sign), and park at the Visitor Center. Or connect to the MUNI #28 bus from downtown.

COURSE

Jog downhill, then (L) on Lincoln Blvd. (Golden Gate Bridge sign). Beyond the bridge viewing area, turn (L) at No Bicycles sign onto Washington Blvd. Where Washington ends at Arguello, go straight. Just before Arguello leaves the Presidio, take a sharp (L) onto the trail alongside West Pacific Ave., down to a ballfield, then up to a lamppost-bordered path. Turn (L) onto this unmarked trail (Lovers' Lane), which descends .5 mile until you turn (R) on MacArthur, (R) on Presidio Blvd., (L) on Lincoln Blvd., and (L) on Montgomery (Visitor Center sign) to finish the loop.

FOOT NOTES

The course starts by winding above the bay on gently rolling terrain for 1.4 miles, between the quiet of the San Francisco National Military Cemetery and the traffic noise of the Golden Gate Bridge approach ramps. Following the toughest, .8-mile-long hill of the route is a fairly level 1.8 miles through woods and past Presidio Golf Course.

On West Pacific Ave., you pass stately homes in the Presidio Heights district, then do a free fall down Lovers' Lane, which got its name when off-duty U.S. soldiers used it to walk into San Francisco to meet their sweethearts.

In the last few blocks you will pass the busy Main Post hospitals, barracks, and Parade Ground. To illustrate how much this former Army base has changed, one of the old barracks is now the Thoreau Center for Sustainability.

The Lands End and Baker Beach route can be tacked on from the intersection of Lincoln Blvd. and Washington for a hilly but spectacular total of 13.0 miles. For info and map, contact Presidio Visitor Information Center, 415-561-4323.

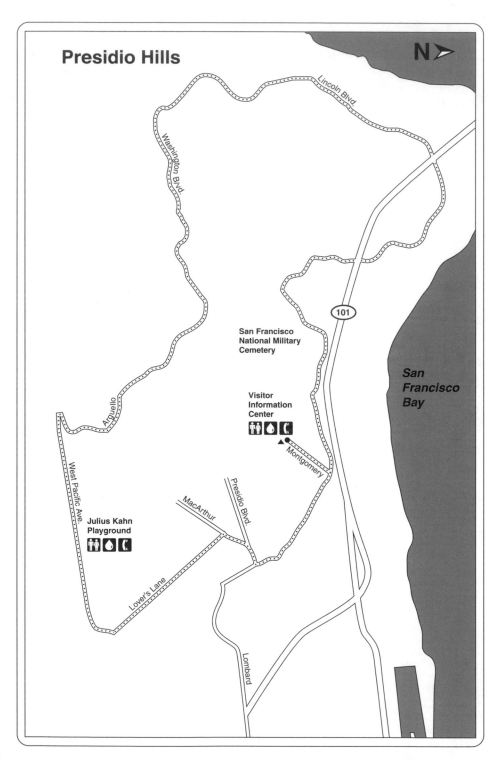

Presidio Hills

N

Lincoln Blvd

Washington Blvd.

101

San Francisco National Military Cemetery

San Francisco Bay

Visitor Information Center

Arguello

Montgomery

West Pacific Ave.

MacArthur

Presidio Blvd.

Julius Kahn Playground

Lover's Lane

Lombard

LANDS END AND BAKER BEACH

8.0 MILES	ROAD/SAND	SCENERY RATING	
	👫 💧	HILL RATING	

Trail running in San Francisco? Indeed, there are rugged trails atop 200-foot bluffs on the northern rim of the city that rival any at Big Sur or Mendocino. The Coastal Trail is a combination of paths, old military roads, a beach, residential sidewalks, and the roadbed of an 1888 steam railroad. What you will remember, however, are the soaring cliffs.

ACCESS

From downtown, go north on Van Ness Ave., (L) on Lombard, (R) on Lincoln Blvd. (in Presidio National Park), and (R) on Ralston Ave. Go 100 meters and park on the (L) at Battery Boutelle sign. Or, connect to the MUNI #28 bus from downtown.

COURSE

Follow the Coastal Trail (there is a sign on the south end of the parking lot) and watch for signposts with a brown backpacker icon as you run away from the Golden Gate Bridge. After .25 mile, the trail runs alongside Lincoln Blvd. Proceed to the next trail sign at a white gate; turn (R) down this dirt road toward Baker Beach. Bear to the (L) along a chain-link fence to the sand and go (L) at the waves. At the drainage stream, turn (L); at the wooden steps, turn (R). The 50 steps bring you up to the ritzy Seacliff neighborhood. Go 50 meters, (L) on 25th Ave.-North, (R) on Sea Cliff/El Camino Del Mar. Just past 32nd Ave., turn (R) at Lands End trailhead sign. The cliff-hugging trail ends at El Camino Del Mar and Point Lobos Ave. Cross the street to Sutro Heights Park. Run the broad dirt road to the end, turn (R), then (L), to complete a P-shaped loop in the park. Head back.

FOOT NOTES

Significant hills include a steady, 1,200-meter plunge to Baker Beach in the first mile; a moderate, 600-meter street climb at 2.0 miles; and a steep rise and subsequent descent on 250 wooden stairs at 3.0 miles, all of which you will do in reverse on the way back. The loose footing makes the course even tougher—good training for the Dipsea Trail Race (see chapter 5).

Along the way, amid cypress trees, you are treated to million-dollar views of the Pacific Ocean and the Golden Gate. (The scenery changes to multi-million-dollar mansions in the Seacliff neighborhood.) Be careful when admiring the views. The trails are wide most of the way, but there are spots where daydreaming would cost you more than a turned ankle.

The .5-mile spin through Sutro Heights Park serves as a pleasant halfway respite from the hilly trails. Former Mayor Adolph Sutro donated this park to the city a century ago, and the stone walls, statues, garden areas, and gazebo are still there, as are stunning views of Ocean Beach.

Marathoners may wish to add the Ocean Beach and Dunes or Lower Golden Gate Park route to make a really tough course. For info, call GGNRA, 415-556-0560.

DR. JOAN'S PRESCRIPTION

Dr. Joan Ullyot ran the Lands End trail for years. "I lived within a block of El Camino Del Mar," she says, "and ran out to Sutro Heights Park and back almost every day." Joan is the author of three books on women's running, a speaker at running symposiums, and a former national-class marathoner.

"I liked the course for its variety. It's pretty wild and never boring; the mixture of fog and sunlight was always a little different." She adds one cautionary note, "It's kind of deserted, so run with a dog or a friend, or carry pepper spray. And keep your eyes open. There are some strange characters out there."

Joan continues to run on scenic trails, but without the ocean view; she now lives in Aspen, Colorado.

TIP

The best time to run this course is midday when the sun is out. Morning and evening fog make the rugged trail portions a little creepy and deprive you of the spectacular views.

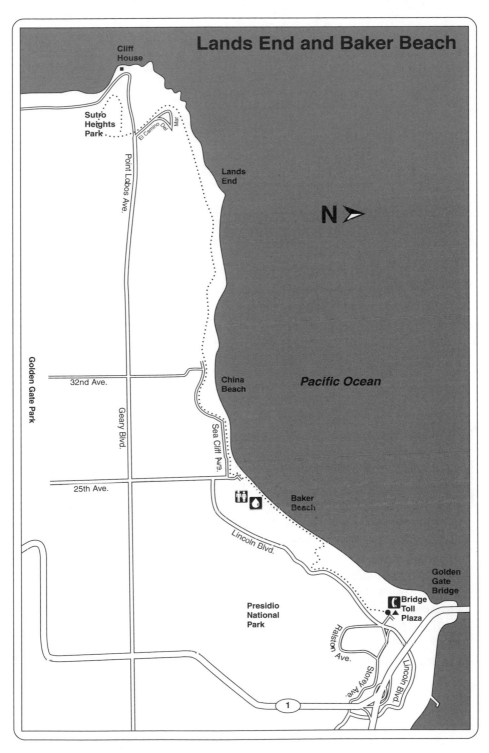

Lands End and Baker Beach

Cliff House

Sutro Heights Park

El Camino Del Mar

Point Lobos Ave.

Lands End

N ➤

Golden Gate Park

32nd Ave.

Geary Blvd.

Sea Cliff Ave.

China Beach

Pacific Ocean

25th Ave.

Baker Beach

Lincoln Blvd.

Presidio National Park

Golden Gate Bridge

Bridge Toll Plaza

Ralston Ave.

Storey Ave.

Lincoln Blvd.

1

UPPER GOLDEN GATE PARK

3.9 MILES	ROAD/TRAIL	SCENERY RATING	
		HILL RATING	

Golden Gate Park has a split personality. The generally flat upper half is a sensory feast, packed with people and filled with the attractions that attract them—museums, botanical gardens, athletic fields, and more. This will be your favorite half if you like to watch people during a flat, easy run.

ACCESS

Driving north into Golden Gate Park from 19th Ave., take the first (R) at Martin Luther King Jr. Dr. After .2 mile, turn (L) on Stow Lake Dr. and go .6 mile around the lake to park at the boathouse or next to the lake. Or, from downtown take the N-Judah trolley to 19th Ave., run two blocks north to King Dr., and turn (R) to Stow Lake. This adds a mile to the run.

COURSE

Main Route. From the boathouse, run away from the lake (downhill) for 100 meters on Stow Lake Dr., turn (R) on John F. Kennedy Dr., and, at Stanyan St. stoplight, cross to the park's block-wide panhandle, bordered by Fell St. and Oak St. Run on the grass or paved path to the end of this eight-block-long peninsula of grass. Turn back, re-cross Stanyan St., continue straight on Kennedy Dr., turn (L) on Middle Dr. (across from the Conservatory of Flowers). Stay on Middle Dr., which bears (R) at AIDS Memorial Grove sign, to its end at King Dr. Turn (R), then (R) again at Stow Lake sign. Go clockwise on the lake's footpath to the boathouse.

Alternate Route (9.6 miles). Add the hilly Lower Golden Gate Park route.

FOOT NOTES

Choose between paved paths or grass for most of this course, which shares turf with Bay to Breakers, the Run to the Far Side, and the San Francisco Marathon. The only real hill is a modest, .25-mile rise up King Dr. to Stow Lake in the last mile. You finish alongside the flat and serene donut-shaped lake where young lovers paddle rowboats and families feed the ducks. Afterward, options include a boat rental at Stow Lake, picnicking, and seeing the park's sights at a slower pace. For info, call 415-751-2766.

KICKIN' AT KEZAR

There are numerous all-weather tracks in the Bay Area, most of them on college campuses, but which one has a Mondo surface and stays open to the public daily from 6:30 A.M. to 9:30 P.M.? Which one has its stadium lights turned on after dark? Which one is situated in a huge urban park where you can do a warm-up jog before a track workout?

The answer is Kezar. In the 1980s, the former home of the San Francisco 49ers was converted from a dilapidated, underused football stadium into a comfortable, 10,000-seat multi-use stadium with a track. The freestanding columns and flagpoles that border the stadium, now used for track meets and the San Francisco Marathon finish, give it a classic feel.

The stadium is located in the park, just two blocks off this route. At the AIDS Memorial Grove, go straight onto Bowling Green Dr. Make the next sharp (L), and then cross Kezar Dr. at the stoplight to the stadium. Several Bay Area clubs use the track for weekly workouts, including the DSE Runners, West Valley, and the Impalas. Most clubs welcome guests, or you can do your own workout.

The bleachers keep most of the evening winds out, and the surroundings are pleasant, consisting of Victorian homes and the University of California Medical Center high-rises. This setting has been the backdrop for many a great workout, and it can be for yours, too.

TIP

Every Sunday, the first third of this course on Kennedy Dr. is closed to auto traffic. Enjoy taking over the street!

LOWER GOLDEN GATE PARK

5.7 MILES	ROAD/TRAIL	SCENERY RATING					
	👫 💧 ☎	HILL RATING					

The lower half of Golden Gate Park appeals to contemplative sorts—runners who want to escape the noise, commotion, and sensory overload of the city. The lower half is hillier, foggier, and lonelier than the upper half, but nature offers much to behold: ponds, dense groves of trees, two windmills, and the ocean.

ACCESS

Driving north into Golden Gate Park from 19th Ave., take the first (R) at King Dr. After .2 mile turn (L) on Stow Lake Dr. Proceed .6 mile around the lake; park at the boathouse or next to the lake. Or, from downtown take the N-Judah trolley to 19th Ave., run two blocks north and turn (R) on King Dr. to get to Stow Lake. This adds a mile to the run.

COURSE

Main Route. From the boathouse, run counterclockwise around the lake on the footpath until it separates from Stow Lake Dr. Follow the road 100 meters downhill to King Dr. Turn (R) onto the well-maintained paved and dirt paths alongside King Dr. or the more primitive, meandering horse trails on your (L), and continue to the Great Hwy. Cross the street to run on the sand or the beach promenade for the next .5 mile. At Dutch Windmill (Kennedy Dr.), turn (R) and follow the paved or dirt paths along Kennedy, which after .5 mile veer (L). Shortly after cresting a 2-mile-long climb, turn (R) on Stow Lake Dr. and charge 100 meters up to the boathouse.

Alternate Route (9.6 miles). Add the Upper Golden Gate Park route for extra distance.

FOOT NOTES

After the first .5 mile this course is all downhill to the beach, then almost all uphill from the beach to the finish. Fortunately, most of the grades are gradual, with the fifth mile the only real toughie.

The lower half of the park has probably been used for more race courses over the years than any site outside Central Park, including the Bay to Breakers 12K, the San Francisco Marathon, and two U.S. Cross-Country Championships. The last 2.5 miles of the route comprise the final third of the Bay to Breakers course; the park's quiet lower half is prized by cross-country runners for its soft, undulating horse trails, huge grass fields, and cool weather. For info, call 415-751-2766.

STRAWBERRY HILL

Strawberry Hill, in the middle of Stow Lake, is an excellent, .3-mile dirt ascent for hill-repetition workouts. "The footing is smooth and the degree of incline is moderate, so you can develop power as you push your way up," notes Mike Fanelli. The 2:25 marathoner has prescribed Strawberry Hill repeats for his running-club charges off and on for 20 years. He adds: "The dirt is soft enough that jogging back down it for the next one isn't too jarring."

After jogging one or two times around the lake (1 mile per loop), go to your (L) from the boathouse about .1 mile to the footbridge, cross and turn (R). After .1 mile of level ground, the terrain starts to rise. At the pond near the top, make a hard (L) and push it up the last, steep 50 meters to the top.

The summit offers a splendid view of the ocean, the bay, the city, and Stow Lake below you. You can jog back down the same way and do several of these climbs, or you can shorten the time back to the start by taking the stone stairs down from the hilltop reservoir. A few times up and down this hill and you'll be ready to flatten the Hayes St. hill at the next Bay to Breakers.

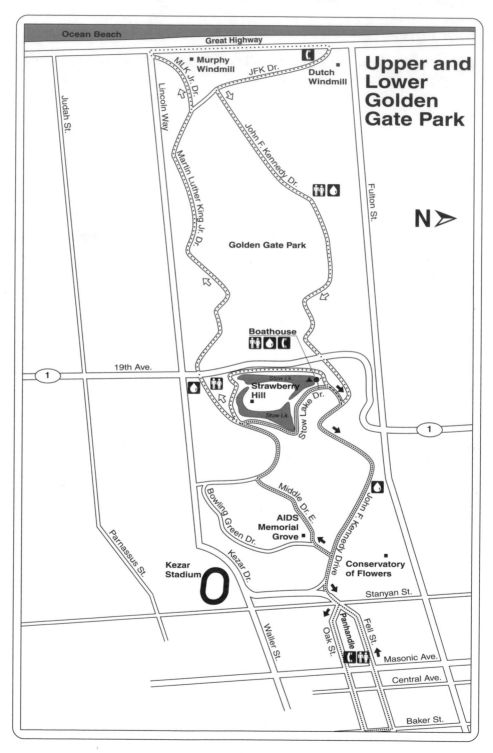

Upper and Lower Golden Gate Park

Ocean Beach
Great Highway

Murphy Windmill
JFK Dr.
Dutch Windmill

MLK Jr. Dr.
Lincoln Way
Martin Luther King Jr. Dr.
John F. Kennedy Dr.
Fulton St.
Judah St.

Golden Gate Park

N

Boathouse

19th Ave.

Stow Lk.
Strawberry Hill
Stow Lk.
Stow Lake Dr.

Middle Dr. E.

Bowling Green Dr.
AIDS Memorial Grove

John F. Kennedy Drive
Conservatory of Flowers

Parnassus St.
Kezar Stadium
Kezar Dr.
Waller St.
Oak St.
Panhandle
Stanyan St.
Fell St.
Masonic Ave.
Central Ave.
Baker St.

OCEAN BEACH AND DUNES

9.4 MILES	ROAD/SAND	SCENERY RATING	
	🚻 💧 ☎	HILL RATING	

If San Francisco singles all took the long walks on the beach that they mention in personal ads, the city's longest and widest beach would be packed every day, not just during rare heat waves. There are enough Ocean Beach walkers to make you feel safe, but not so many that they detract from the solitary pleasure of beach running.

ACCESS

From downtown, drive out Geary Blvd. to the end, turn (R) on 48th Ave., (L) on Point Lobos Ave., and park in the lot on the (R) at the bottom of the hill. Or take the L-Taraval trolley from downtown to the end of the line at Ocean Beach. This brings you to the midpoint of the route, which you can split into two out-and-backs.

COURSE

Start running south on the beach or on the concrete beach promenade. There are two windmills on the (L); cut across the beach to the second one and at the stoplight cross Great Hwy. to the bike path. Follow it or its hard-packed-sand shoulder to the end at Sloat Blvd., then cross at the light to the beach. Run on the sand for about a mile to the sand trail that heads up into the dunes just before you reach the highest cliffs. A two-minute walk or tough run brings you up to a paved bike path; turn (R) and then (R) again at the paved road. This soon becomes a bike path again; continue uphill and turn (L) at the Battery Davis sign. Across the parking lot, descend 100 stairs at the Beach Access sign (where hang gliders push off) and continue down the sand path to the beach. Turn (R) and head all the way back to the start on any combination of beach, bike path, or promenade, all of which parallel the shore.

FOOT NOTES

This route is an under-used treasure. You'll enjoy the crunch of sand dollars and seaweed under your feet on the beach, and the sight of pelicans and hang gliders in the sky. The Fort Funston dunes are a preserved reminder of the dunes that once covered the western third of the city.

This is also a flexible route. For most of the way there is a choice of surfaces, from hard concrete to soft sand, and you can lengthen the distance to 15 to 18 miles by tacking on the Lake Merced, Lands End and Baker Beach, or Lower Golden Gate Park routes, which all come within a few blocks of intersecting this one. Or, you can follow the beach for miles beyond the route turnaround, all the way to Pacifica at low tide. For info, call 415-556-0560 or 415-239-2366.

LIFE IS A BEACH

Beach running is not only exhilarating, it's great training. I got into the best shape of my life while running on the beach five days a week. To make this run a quality workout, push it occasionally as you would in an interval or fartlek session on the soft-sand interior of the beach; your heartbeat will soar. Another option is to run repetitions up any of the sand trails in Fort Funston at the route turnaround.

This high-octane workout will strengthen lungs, calves, ankles, and muscles you didn't know you had, but don't overdo it. Otherwise, your over-extended Achilles tendons will ache for days.

If you become such a beach-running convert that you start checking the daily tide chart in the *Chronicle*, you won't want to miss the Ocean Beach Run. Held every spring at extreme low tide, the 5K and 10K are run entirely on Ocean Beach, starting at Sloat Blvd. Call 415-589-7417.

TIP

This is the best dog-running route of any in the book because there are no traffic problems. Your pooch will love the beach, but must be on a leash.

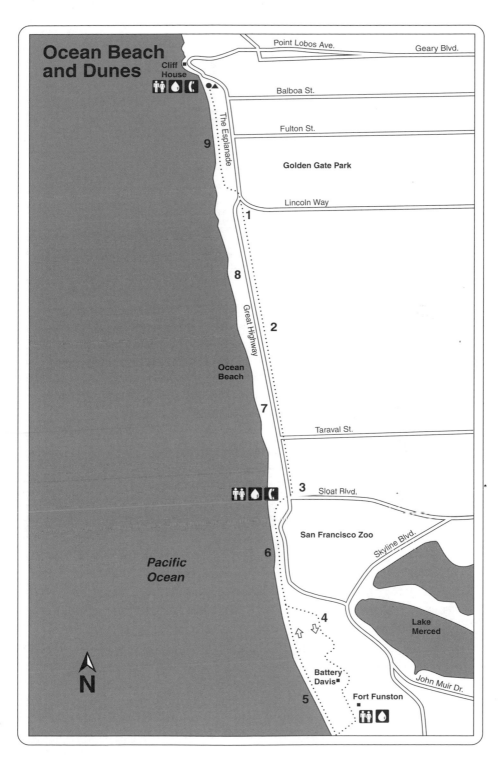

Ocean Beach
and Dunes

Point Lobos Ave.

Geary Blvd.

Cliff
House

Balboa St.

The Esplanade

9

Fulton St.

Golden Gate Park

Lincoln Way

1

8

Great Highway

2

Ocean
Beach

7

Taraval St.

3

Sloat Blvd.

San Francisco Zoo

Skyline Blvd.

6

Pacific
Ocean

4

Lake
Merced

Battery
Davis

John Muir Dr.

5

Fort Funston

N

LAKE MERCED LOOP

4.8 MILES 👫 💧 ☏	ROAD/TRAIL	SCENERY RATING	HILL RATING

This route is strictly no frills and no hills by San Francisco standards. It's a simple and scenic loop around a lake and alongside two golf courses, with no street crossings. Enough fellow runners and walkers share the course to keep you from getting bored.

ACCESS

From downtown, take Hwy. 101-South, I-280-South, John Daly Blvd. exit, west to (R) on Lake Merced Blvd., (L) on John Muir Dr., (R) on Skyline Blvd., and (R) on Harding Blvd. at the Lake Merced/Harding Park sign. Park at the Boathouse Restaurant. Or take BART to Balboa Park station, and MUNI bus #88 to the lake.

COURSE

Main route. Head out Harding Blvd. to Skyline Blvd., and turn (R) on the bike path. Proceed clockwise around the lake on the bike path or its dirt shoulder. Turn (R) on Harding Blvd. to finish.

Alternate route (10.1 miles). Run the main route for .7 mile, then turn (L) onto Sunset Blvd. The distance is 5.3 miles to the end of Sunset at King Dr. in Golden Gate Park and back. Choose between the wide dirt path on the east shoulder or the paved path on the west shoulder. On returning to the lake, turn (L) on the bike path and complete the loop. For a 15.8-miler, turn (L) onto King Dr. and add the Lower Golden Gate Park loop.

FOOT NOTES

The hills are long and steady, but tame. The mild inclines are in the first and last quarters of the course and the downhills are in the middle.

Dogs on leashes are fine. A cycling speed limit of 10 MPH keeps aggressive cyclists away. There are exercise stations in the first mile. After your run, you can enjoy a view of the lake from the Boathouse Restaurant or the adjacent picnicking lawn.

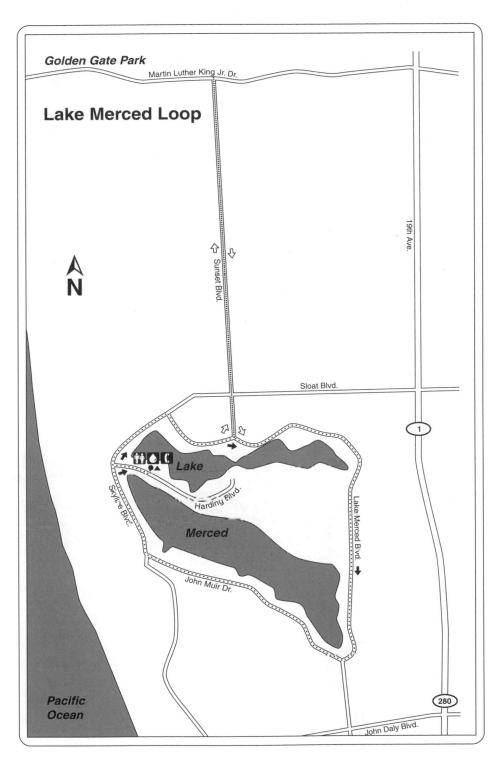

NORTH BAY

The blue peak of Tamalpais . . . blue as a sapphire on the paler azure of the sky, spoke to us of wider outlooks and the bright Pacific. For Tamalpais stands sentry, like a lighthouse, over the Golden Gates, between the bay and the open ocean, and looks down indifferently on both.

—*Robert Louis Stevenson*

Her name, pronounced "Tam-ul-PIE-us," combines the Coast Miwok Indian words for coast (*tamal*) and mountain (*pais*). In more recent times she has been dubbed "The Sleeping Maiden" for the shape formed by her three 2,500-foot peaks. If the comparison can be furthered, you could say an oversized, crocheted blanket of red-earth trails covers her. The blanket spreads south to the Golden Gate, west to the beaches and ocean cliffs, north to the tip of Point Reyes, and east to the lapping inlets of San Francisco Bay. On the eastern fringe are Marin County's only substantial towns, which in sum occupy a small portion of the county's wide-open spaces.

This is trail-running heaven. There may not be another small suburban county in America with as fine an array of trail running choices as Marin County. The trails sprawl over 150,000 acres of public parklands—nearly half the county—which is why most of Marin's runners are trail regulars.

The climate is a bonus: warm summers that seldom get unbearably hot and cool winters that rarely get cold enough for gloves. Apart from rainstorms, which are more pronounced the closer you get to Tam's peaks, there is seldom anything to stop you from enjoying a run any day of the year.

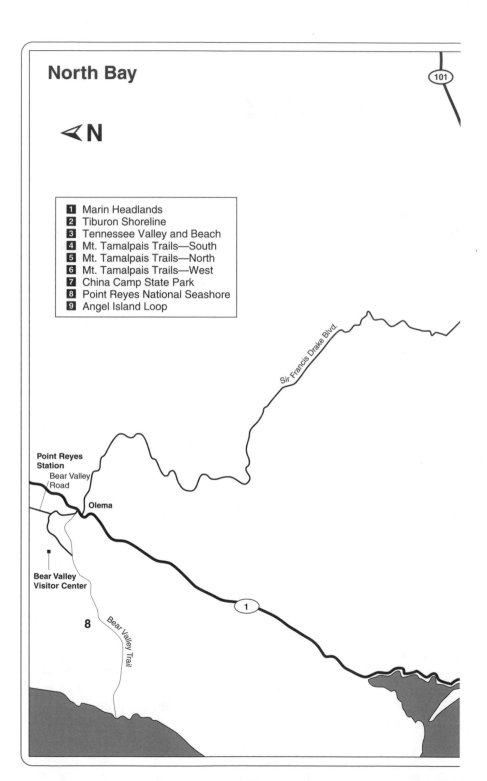

North Bay

⊲N

1 Marin Headlands
2 Tiburon Shoreline
3 Tennessee Valley and Beach
4 Mt. Tamalpais Trails—South
5 Mt. Tamalpais Trails—North
6 Mt. Tamalpais Trails—West
7 China Camp State Park
8 Point Reyes National Seashore
9 Angel Island Loop

101

Sir Francis Drake Blvd.

Point Reyes Station
Bear Valley Road
Olema

Bear Valley Visitor Center

8
Bear Valley Trail

1

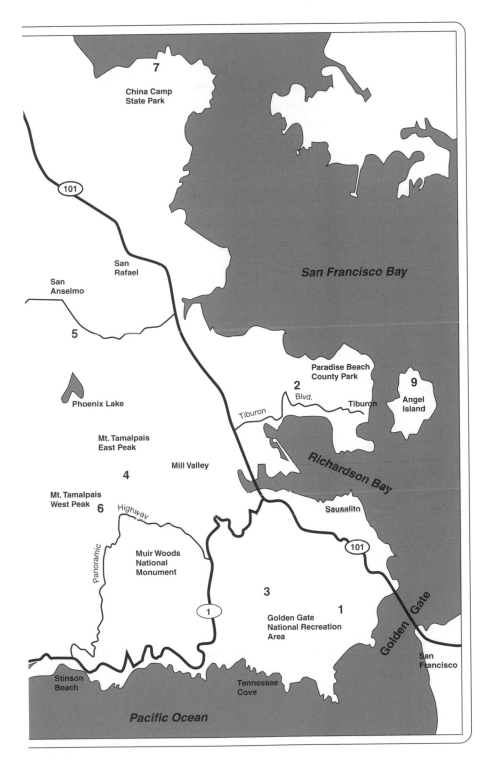

7

China Camp
State Park

101

San
Rafael

San
Anselmo

5

Phoenix Lake

Mt. Tamalpais
East Peak

Mill Valley

San Francisco Bay

Paradise Beach
County Park

2

Blvd.

Tiburon

Tiburon

9

Angel
Island

4

Mt. Tamalpais
West Peak

6

Highway

Panoramic

Muir Woods
National
Monument

Richardson Bay

Sausalito

101

1

3

Golden Gate
National Recreation
Area

1

Golden Gate

San
Francisco

Stinson
Beach

Tennessee
Cove

Pacific Ocean

TRANSIT

All of these routes are easiest to reach by car except, of course, the Angel Island Loop. Only one route (Mt. Tamalpais Trails–North) is accessible at any time from San Francisco or from elsewhere in Marin. During weekday commute hours, buses from San Francisco stop at the start and finish of the Tiburon Shoreline (#8 bus) and Mt. Tamalpais Trails–South (#4 bus) routes. On weekends, Mt. Tamalpais Trails–West is accessible on the #63 bus and Point Reyes on the #65 bus. Call Golden Gate Transit at 415-453-2100 or 415-817-1717 for a map or timetable info.

MARIN HEADLANDS

8.2 MILES	ROAD/TRAIL	SCENERY RATING	
		HILL RATING	

In a pioneering victory for parkland preservation, unpopulated Gerbode Valley was rescued from the bulldozer in 1966 when plans to build a "beautiful planned community" of 25,000 were defeated. That triumph ultimately led to the Golden Gate National Recreation Area, of which the 12,000-acre Marin Headlands is the biggest chunk.

Runners, hikers, and mountain bikers adore the Headlands for its proximity to San Francisco, its stunning views of the Pacific Ocean and Golden Gate, and the soft, red soil of its 50 miles of well-marked trails. You can explore additional trails after this challenging introduction to the area.

ACCESS

Drive Hwy. 101-North to first exit north of the Golden Gate Bridge (Sausalito); make an immediate (L) at Marin Headlands sign; go under the freeway and take first (R) on Conzelman Rd.—the most spectacular 1.1 miles of winding road you'll ever drive—to first (R) on McCullough. Go .9 mile to the end, turn (L) on Bunker Rd., and drive 2.2 miles to Rodeo Beach parking lot.

COURSE

Run back on the road you drove in on (Bunker Rd.), past pelican-packed Rodeo Lagoon, for .6 mile. Where the road bears (R) across the lagoon, go straight at the trailhead sign onto Miwok Trail. After .4 mile, bear (R) on Bobcat Trail, climb about 800 elevation-feet in approximately 3.1 miles, then turn (R) down Miwok Trail (20 yards past Miwok Trail North sign) to complete the loop. At the bottom, head back to your car.

FOOT NOTES

My wife hiked this route through grasslands, chaparral, and wildflowers with me when she was nine days past her due date—and gave birth to our first child the next day. No wonder. The climb up Bobcat Trail makes anyone labor. After a mostly level first mile to the Miwok and Bobcat Trail fork, it's up, up, and up—gradually, moderately, and steeply—for 3.1 miles, except for a couple of short, steep descents. This is great training for the Dipsea Trail Race (see chapter 5).

At the high point, where the Bobcat and Miwok Trails converge, you reach a tall, white monolith (an FAA flight navigation marker) that you can see all the way up. Fortunately, it's all downhill the rest of the way.

You may spot a bobcat, on the Bobcat Trail, as I did! For information, call the Headlands Visitor Center at 415-331-1540.

DAY TRIPPING

The Headlands is a superb day trip destination. After the run, you can use the showers at the finish (by the restrooms) and picnic on spacious Rodeo Beach, which attracts a blend of families, couples, and surfers. It's a short drive from the beach to the Headlands Visitor Center, Point Bonita Lighthouse, the Bay Area Discovery Museum, and the Sausalito waterfront. The closest attraction, however, is The Marine Mammal Center (TMMC).

Even if you miss the sign for the TMMC on Bunker Rd., you will hear the barking sea lions. For no charge, visitors can observe them and other sea creatures that have been rescued from northern California beaches, as they are nursed back to health. Runners help keep the TMMC afloat. About $30,000 is raised each year at the Run for the Seals 4 Mile. The race course shares the first and last .5 mile with this route, but stays mostly on flat and rolling paved roads. There is always a multitude of food and prizes. If you are interested, the race is on the first Sunday in March and draws about 1,500 runners and walkers. For info, contact TMMC, GGNRA-Marin Headlands, Sausalito, CA 94965; phone 415-289-SEAL; http://www.tmmc.org/.

TIP

Like most coastal mountain routes, the weather is fluky. It can be foggy at the beach and hot on the ridge, or vice versa, so carry water and tie a windbreaker around your waist.

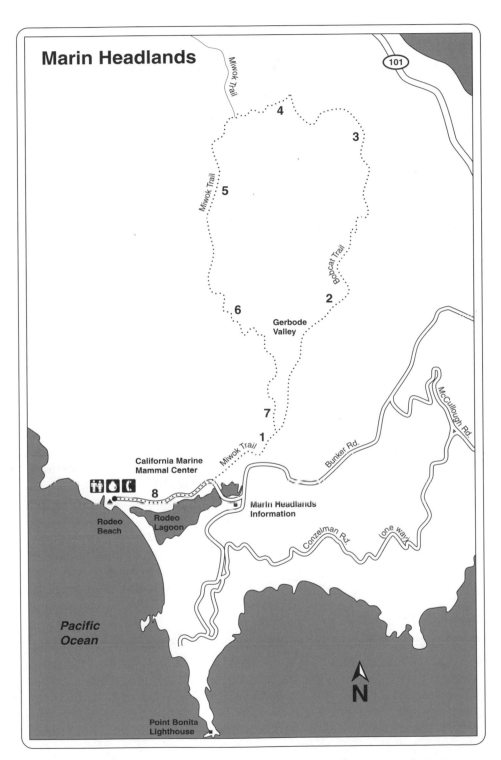

Marin Headlands

101

Miwok Trail

4

3

Miwok Trail

5

Bobcat Trail

6

Gerbode
Valley

2

7

1

Miwok Trail

California Marine
Mammal Center

8

Marin Headlands
Information

Rodeo
Beach

Rodeo
Lagoon

Bunker Rd.

McCullough Rd.

Conzelman Rd.

lone way

Pacific
Ocean

N

Point Bonita
Lighthouse

TIBURON SHORELINE

5.0 MILES	ROAD/TRAIL	SCENERY RATING	
	🚻 💧 ☎	HILL RATING	

Many San Francisco lawyers live in Tiburon because it is insulated from the bustle of San Francisco, yet close. Seeming to float on the fog bank that clings to the bay are the city's skyscrapers and the Golden Gate Bridge.

ACCESS

Drive Hwy. 101-North to 6 miles north of the Golden Gate Bridge; exit at Tiburon Blvd.; turn (R) and proceed 1.5 miles on Tiburon. Turn (R) on Blackie's Pasture Rd.; park. Or, take a Red & White Ferry (800-BAY-CRUISE) from San Francisco's Pier 43-1/2 to Tiburon and run the main course backwards. Conclude the trip with brunch on the bay.

COURSE

Main Route. From the bronze statue of Blackie (the beloved horse who grazed this meadow from 1941 to 1966), follow the bike path or parallel dirt path from the parking lot to downtown Tiburon. Stay on Tiburon Blvd. for another .5 mile until you reach the trendy restaurant row on Main St. Head back to the start.

Alternate Route (8.6 miles). Beyond Main St., continue on Tiburon Blvd. (which becomes Paradise Dr.) and follow it around scenic Tiburon peninsula. Stop to explore Paradise Beach Park if you wish. Once you've covered a total of 8.0 miles, turn (L) at Trestle Glen Dr. and proceed to its end at the bike path across Tiburon Blvd. Turn (R) to return to your car.

FOOT NOTES

The heavily-used main route is essentially traffic-free and flat, hugging the shoreline alongside kite-flying fields and tennis courts. The long route is rolling, curving and narrow, but shady and gorgeous.

Downtown Tiburon is a smaller but hipper version of Sausalito. Nature-minded tourists may want to visit the Audubon Center (376 Greenwood Beach Dr., 415-388-2524), a few blocks west of Blackie's Pasture.

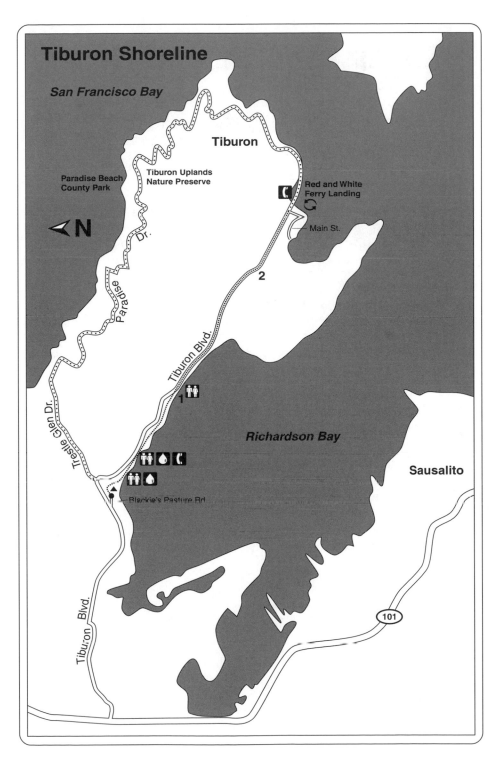

Tiburon Shoreline

San Francisco Bay

Tiburon

Paradise Beach
County Park

Tiburon Uplands
Nature Preserve

Red and White
Ferry Landing

Paradise Dr.

N

Main St.

2

Tiburon Blvd.

1

Trestle Glen Dr.

Richardson Bay

Sausalito

Blackie's Pasture Rd.

Tiburon Blvd.

101

TENNESSEE VALLEY AND BEACH

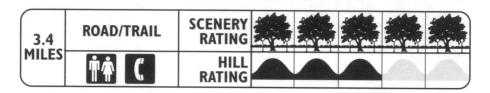

3.4 MILES	ROAD/TRAIL	SCENERY RATING	
	🚻 📞	HILL RATING	

Just five minutes off the freeway, this is a convenient and delightful getaway run. The narrow valley between imposing ridges, with few signs of civilization, confers a sense of privacy. Eucalyptus and wildflowers line the trail.

ACCESS

Drive Hwy. 101-North to 4 miles north of the Golden Gate Bridge; exit at Hwy. 1 (toward Stinson Beach); after .6 mile turn (L) on Tennessee Valley Rd. Park immediately on the right shoulder to start Alternate Route, or drive 1.7 miles to the end at a parking lot for Main Route.

COURSE

Main Route. At the trail-map kiosk, head down paved Tennessee Valley Trail for .6 mile. At the unmarked fork, bear (R) onto the dirt road (the paved left fork takes you onto a working ranch). After .2 mile, keep (R) on the wider high branch of the trail until it reconnects with the low branch .6 mile later. Continue to the beach. On the way back, bear (R) at Tennessee Valley Trail split to follow the creek-hugging low trail and return.

Alternate Route (6.8 miles). Double your fun to 6.8 miles by starting the run at the intersection of Hwy. 1 and Tennessee Valley Rd. This adds a quiet and relatively flat stretch of country road, with a dirt shoulder for much of the way.

FOOT NOTES

This route starts with a moderate downhill, then rolls (sometimes steeply) to the beach—a net descent of about 200 elevation-feet. The return trip is a steady, gradual incline.

Stop to enjoy the mid-sized beach at Tennessee Cove, framed by high cliffs, but don't even think about taking a dip. The steamship *Tennessee* was shipwrecked here in 1853, so you can imagine what the surf would do to a mere runner. After the run, stretch or snack at the picnic area. For info, call the Headlands Visitor Center at 415-331-1540.

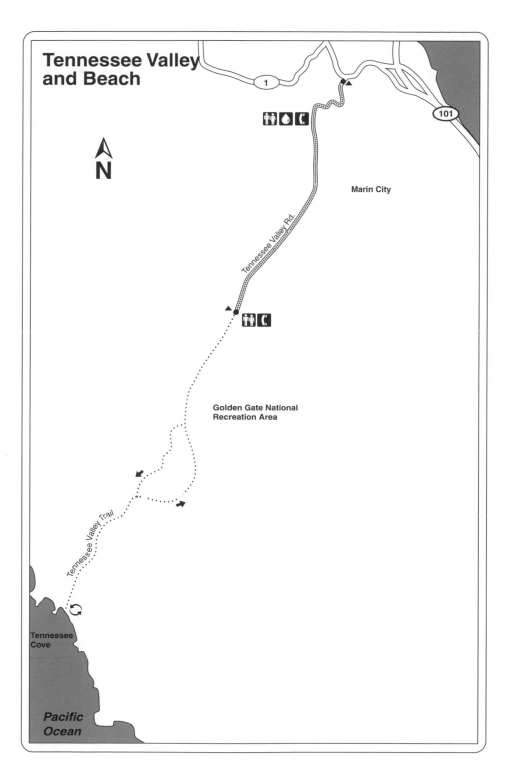

Tennessee Valley and Beach

N

1

101

Marin City

Tennessee Valley Rd.

Golden Gate National Recreation Area

Tennessee Valley Trail

Tennessee Cove

Pacific Ocean

MT. TAMALPAIS TRAILS—SOUTH

10.6 MILES	ROAD/TRAIL [icons]	SCENERY RATING	[mountains rating]
		HILL RATING	[hills rating]

Here is a way to run the slopes of Mt. Tam without driving on any winding roads to the start. The scenery's to die for, and the last 4.2 miles of the course are downhill. The bad news is that the route is out-and-back, so you know what that means about the first 4.2 miles. But hey, if you want flat-and-fast courses, move to Kansas!

ACCESS

Take Hwy. 101-North 6 miles north of the Golden Gate Bridge; exit onto E. Blithedale Ave. (Mill Valley) and turn (L) to cross over the freeway; continue 2.1 miles and park near the intersection of Blithedale and Throckmorton.

COURSE

Run up W. Blithedale 1.2 miles and turn (R) at "Northridge-Blithedale Summit" fire-road gate. Keep straight for .6 mile, then turn (L) at Mt. Tamalpais Watershed fire-road fork. Continue straight on dirt and asphalt (where you are briefly on paved Fern Canyon Rd.) for 2.3 miles to the high point. Two parallel fire roads head downhill; turn (L) on either one (they soon merge) to gradually descend 1.1 miles; turn (L) on Panoramic Hwy. and jog 50 yards to the parking lot across from Mountain Home Inn. Drink in the panorama of Mt. Tam and the ocean; return.

FOOT NOTES

A 1.2-mile gradual rise, a steeper 1.8-mile climb, then another 1.2-mile gradual incline add up to a steady, but not steep, 4.2 miles of climbing. You get to coast most of the way back. Don't be surprised to cross paths with runners training for the Dipsea Race, which isn't much tougher than this course.

On this route Tam, the bay, the ocean, and San Francisco are all visible when it isn't foggy. After your run, walk one block down Throckmorton to the vibrant heart of Mill Valley for a hard-earned latte. For info, call Mt. Tamalpais State Park at 415-388-2070.

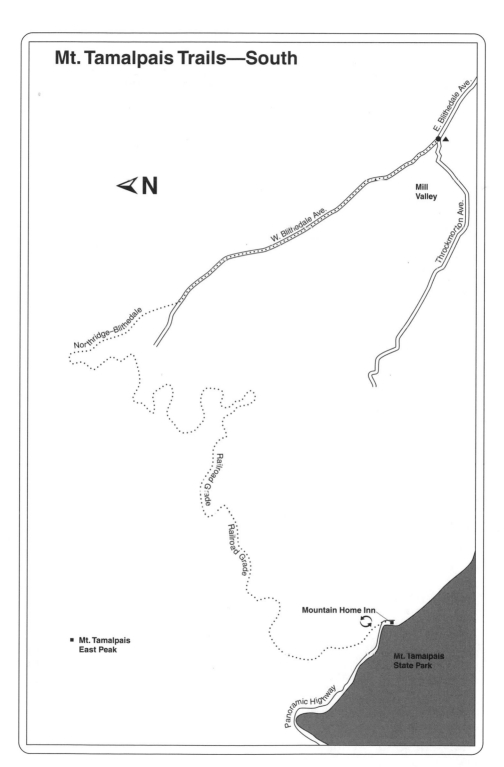

Mt. Tamalpais Trails—South

N

W. Blithedale Ave.

E. Blithedale Ave.

Mill
Valley

Throckmorton Ave.

Northridge–Blithedale

Railroad Grade

Railroad Grade

Mountain Home Inn

■ Mt. Tamalpais
East Peak

Mt. Tamalpais
State Park

Panoramic Highway

MT. TAMALPAIS TRAILS–NORTH

| 5.1 MILES | ROAD/TRAIL | SCENERY RATING | |
| | 🚻 💧 📞 | HILL RATING | |

Road races aren't the only place to find the Bay Area's top runners on Sunday mornings. Scores of them flock to the trails surrounding Phoenix Lake, cradled in the northern foothills of Mt. Tam. They burn up the hills on runs of 12 to 22 miles, zipping past runners, hikers, and mountain bikers with less talent or motivation.

ACCESS

Drive Hwy. 101-North to 9 miles north of the Golden Gate Bridge; exit at Sir Francis Drake Blvd. (toward San Anselmo). After 3.0 miles turn (L) at the stoplight onto Lagunitas Rd. (in Ross). Proceed one block and turn (L) at Ross Common; park on the right.

COURSE

Main Route. Run west on paved Lagunitas Rd. or on parallel dirt path, past the mansions of Ross, then continue straight on dirt road along Phoenix Creek to the parking lot at the end. Turn (R) across the footbridge, climb to Phoenix Dam, turn (L) onto the dam, and run clockwise around the lake. This requires (R) turns at two trail forks— first onto narrow Gertrude Ord Trail (at signpost and wooden stairs), then over a narrow footbridge that brings you back onto a wide fire road (Phoenix Lake sign). You'll pass the century-old Phoenix Lake cabin as you complete the loop to the dam. Then head back to the start.

Alternate Route (11+ miles). Instead of turning (R) onto Phoenix Lake Rd., turn (L) and go west to Shaver Grade Fire Road. Climb steadily (600 elevation-feet in 2 miles) to the upper lakes, Bon Tempe and Lagunitas. Touring the lakes before plunging back down to Phoenix Lake Rd. is a venture requiring fortitude and quite a few turns. Study the trail map posted at Phoenix Dam, or obtain one from the Marin Municipal Water District (415-459-5267) to determine which combination of trails suits your ambitions.

FOOT NOTES

Phoenix is the lowest in a string of five reservoirs, all of them on 20,000 acres of undeveloped watershed lands crisscrossed by 150 miles of trails. The scenery isn't as breathtaking as in adjacent Mt. Tamalpais State Park or Point Reyes National Seashore, but the drive to the start is shorter and there are more runners, hikers, and mountain bikers.

This route is a grab bag of flats and gradual-to-steep ups and downs, with a generally uphill first third, a level and rolling middle (around the lake), and a downhill finish.

TRASON'S FAVORITE TRAILS

Every Sunday morning, Ross Common is packed with the cars of elite runners, from counties outside Marin. The trail running here is that good. The trails are also excellent in the East Bay, where ultramarathon queen Ann Trason lives. So, it's saying something that she makes the trip to Ross once or twice every week.

"There's such diversity on the trails above Phoenix Lake," says Ann, the most accomplished female ultramarathon runner ever. "There are forests, lakes, ferns, and waterfalls, and the trails are remarkably well-maintained." When Ann is training for a trail race like the Western States 100 Mile, in which she has finished second overall, she does a two-hour run on Wednesday evenings and trail romps lasting up to seven hours on Sundays.

For Ann, the variety of intertwining trails is vital. She gushes, "I've run 40-milers up there without repeating the same trail. It's amazing." So is Trason, and don't be too surprised to bump into her in Marin's lake district.

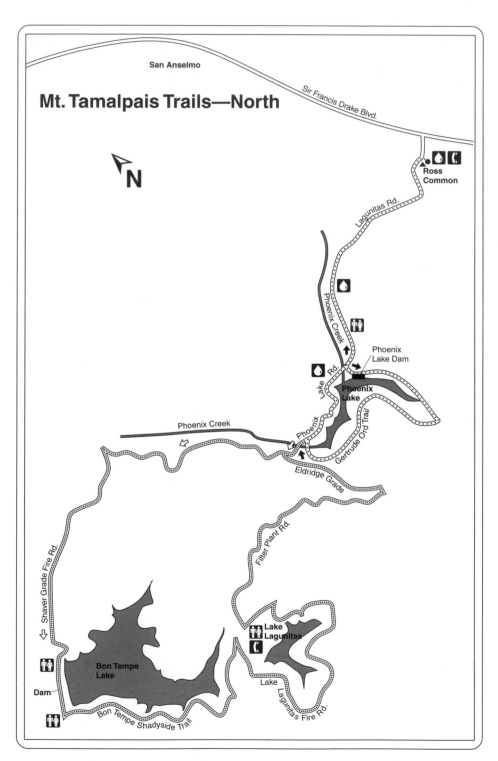

Mt. Tamalpais Trails—North

San Anselmo

Sir Francis Drake Blvd.

N

Ross Common

Lagunitas Rd.

Phoenix Creek

Phoenix Lake Dam

Lake Rd.

Phoenix Lake

Phoenix

Gertrude Ord Trail

Phoenix Creek

Eldridge Grade

Filter Plant Rd.

Shaver Grade Fire Rd.

Lake Lagunitas

Bon Tempe Lake

Dam

Bon Tempe Shadyside Trail

Lake Lagunitas Fire Rd.

MT. TAMALPAIS TRAILS—WEST

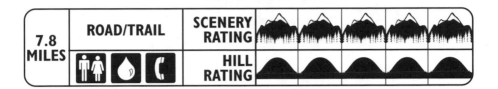

7.8 MILES	ROAD/TRAIL	SCENERY RATING	
	🚻 💧 📞	HILL RATING	

There is tremendous variety on this route. Trails fluctuate between smooth and rocky, wide and narrow. Views range from 50 feet of woods to 50 miles of coastline; vegetation ranges from low brush to towering redwoods. The terrain changes from rugged, mind-bending ascents in the first half to gentle, mesmerizing descents on fern-lined paths.

ACCESS

Drive Hwy. 101-North to 4 miles north of the Golden Gate Bridge; exit onto Hwy. 1 (toward Stinson Beach) and go .8 mile to the first stoplight; turn (L) to stay on Hwy. 1. After 2.7 miles turn (R) onto Panoramic Hwy. (Mt. Tamalpais sign) and go 2.6 miles to the parking lot across from Mountain Home Inn.

COURSE

Just north of the Inn, turn (R) up the paved road to the fire station. Behind the station, go (L) on the dirt road, and just past the water tank, turn (L) up the narrow stairs. Although the trail sign doesn't indicate it, this is Matt Davis Trail. At Nora Trail, turn (R) and go to West Point Inn. Behind the rustic hiking lodge, pick up Rock Spring Trail and proceed to Mountain Theater. At the restrooms beyond the dirt stage, turn (R) down Easy Grade Trail, and (R) again on paved Old Stage Rd. Cross the Panoramic Hwy. to Stapelveldt Trail (behind the Pantoll Ranger Station and its trail map kiosk). From Stapelveldt go straight on the TCC Trail at the bench and straight on Troop 80 Spur Trail at Van Wyck Meadow (Pop. 3 Stellar Jays sign). Turn (L) on paved Alice Eastwood Rd.; go (L) up the stairs (Trestle Trail sign) to the parking lot.

FOOT NOTES

There are only two half-miles you may dislike on this route: the climb up Nora Trail (the steepest sustained grind by far) and the asphalt at the end. What you will like are killer views of the ocean, the bay, the bridges, and San Francisco, and the wooden footbridges over streams and waterfalls. It's a lot like running the Dipsea Trail, but much less taxing.

If you wish to explore any of the remaining 40 miles of trails in 6,700-acre Mt. Tamalpais State Park, call 415-388-2070 for a map.

A LONG-RUNNING TRADITION

If races are the heart of long-distance running and solitary runs are the soul, then group training runs are the spirit. Those that you can count on, in every season and over the years, last because they have something special to offer. The Mountain Home run, has started across from the luxurious inn on Panoramic Hwy. every Saturday at 9:00 A.M. since 1970. The beauty of the converging trails attracts participants in every season.

"In 1970 there were just two of us," recalls Don Pickett, a former Dipsea winner, "but then people started joining us one by one." The weekly turnout has ranged from 15 to 40 runners ever since.

"To my knowledge, not one Saturday run has been skipped," says Pickett. "It's weathered the worst of Marin's storms and the Trailside killer." The mass murderer claimed a victim on the Matt Davis Trail, spooking the Saturday group into running closer together until he was apprehended.

There are two unwritten rules of this long-running tradition. One is that slower runners are allowed to catch up every few miles at water stops. The other is that a discussion about which trails to take prefaces each run. Somehow an agreement is always reached and the route is a bit different almost every week. The course described here is a typical loop.

TIP

Don't start this run without fresh legs, or you risk a turned ankle or a fall on the rocks and roots that lurk like land mines.

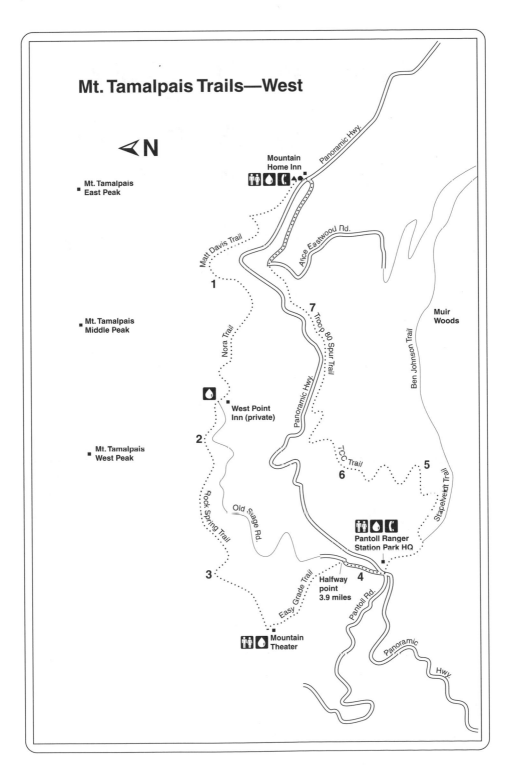

Mt. Tamalpais Trails—West

N

Mt. Tamalpais East Peak

Mt. Tamalpais Middle Peak

Mt. Tamalpais West Peak

Panoramic Hwy.

Mountain Home Inn

Matt Davis Trail

1

Alice Eastwood Rd.

7

Troop 80 Spur Trail

Muir Woods

Nora Trail

Ben Johnson Trail

West Point Inn (private)

Panoramic Hwy.

2

TCC Trail

5

6

Stapelveldt Trail

Rock Spring Trail

Old Stage Rd.

Pantoll Ranger Station Park HQ

3

Easy Grade Trail

Halfway point 3.9 miles

4

Pantoll Rd.

Mountain Theater

Panoramic

Hwy.

CHINA CAMP STATE PARK

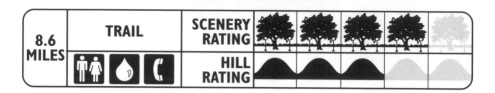

8.6 MILES	TRAIL	SCENERY RATING	
	👫 💧 ☎	HILL RATING	

There are so many spectacular, trail-laced parklands in Marin County that even some locals never make it to 1,640-acre China Camp State Park. They're missing out. The horse trails through oak, eucalyptus, and deciduous trees are well-marked, well-maintained, and uncrowded. Steep ridges to the west literally keep the fog at bay most days.

ACCESS

Drive Hwy. 101-North to 11 miles north of the Golden Gate Bridge; exit at Central San Rafael. Take first (R) onto 2nd St. and go 5.4 miles (the street name changes to 3rd St. and then to Pt. San Pedro Rd.) to China Camp Village sign. Park on the road or in the lot ($3).

COURSE

At the paved lot trailhead, take Village Trail .2 mile and turn (R) on Shoreline Trail. After 4.4 miles turn (L) on Back Ranch Meadows Trail. Walk this .5 mile unless you're a mountain goat; turn (L) on Bay View Trail, (L) on Ridge Trail, (R) on Oak Ridge Trail, (L) on Peacock Gap Trail, and (R) on Shoreline Trail to the finish.

FOOT NOTES

The grades are gradual with the exception of the fifth mile, on Back Ranch Meadows Trail, which gets so steep that walking is advised. This grind, however, rewards you with a long, gradual descent and wonderful views of San Pablo Bay.

After finishing, you may want to visit the free museum located just below the parking lot. China Camp (Wa Jen Ha Lio) is the last surviving Chinese fishing village in America, dating to 1870. Bay shrimp are caught off Pt. San Pedro and sold fresh in the dilapidated snack bar next to the museum. After consuming some history and some shrimp, relax on the adjacent beach. For info and a map, call China Camp State Park at 415-456-0766.

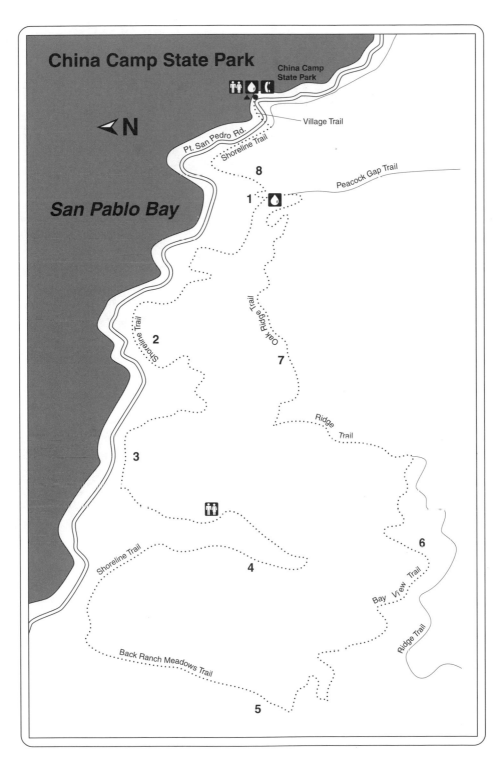

China Camp State Park

China Camp
State Park

San Pablo Bay

N

Pt. San Pedro Rd.

Village Trail

Shoreline Trail

Peacock Gap Trail

Oak Ridge Trail

Ridge Trail

Shoreline Trail

Shoreline Trail

Back Ranch Meadows Trail

Bay View Trail

Ridge Trail

1
2
3
4
5
6
7
8

POINT REYES NATIONAL SEASHORE

8.6 MILES	TRAIL	SCENERY RATING					
		HILL RATING					

There's no finer place to run in the Bay Area than the Point Reyes peninsula, making it well worth the long but pretty drive. With its diversity of terrain and microclimates, Point Reyes National Seashore is home to one-fifth of California's flora and nearly half of North America's bird species. Of greater relevance to runners, its 70 miles of well-marked trails vary from gently rolling coastside paths to soaring climbs into the hills. This route, with its tantalizing blend of cool forest paths and ocean views, is a microcosm of what the peninsula has to offer.

ACCESS

Drive Hwy. 101-North to 9 miles north of the Golden Gate Bridge; exit onto Sir Francis Drake Blvd. (toward San Anselmo) and drive 21 miles to the village of Olema. Turn (R) on Hwy. 1 for one block, and then (L) at Point Reyes National Seashore sign onto Bear Valley Rd. After .5 mile, turn (L) at Seashore HQ sign and follow the road .2 mile to Bear Valley Visitor Center.

COURSE

Start at the Bear Valley trailhead at the south end of the parking lot. Stay on Bear Valley Trail for 4.0 miles; bear (L) onto Coast Trail (toward Wildcat Camp), which proceeds for .3 mile to Arch Rock. Take a rest; head back.

FOOT NOTES

Most of this run along Coast Creek is on a smooth and shaded fire road, 5 to 10 feet wide, bordered by mature aspens, evergreens, ferns, and wildflowers.

The first 1.7 miles is a gradual to moderate incline to deer-populated Divide Meadow, where Teddy Roosevelt once hunted. This divides the run into easy and difficult quarters. Most of the next 2.6 miles are gently downhill to the turnaround at Arch Rock. The Rock is a marvelous spot replete with crashing surf and spectacular views.

You can pick up a map inside the Visitor Center or study the map posted outside the entrance if you have time for further explorations. If this course isn't challenging enough, consider adding a few extra miles in either direction on the Coast Trail. It meanders for miles on rolling terrain, both north and south from the Bear Valley Trail near Arch Rock.

Inside the Visitor Center you can take in the natural history displays or watch a short film on the seashore. I also recommend a stroll across the parking lot to a wondrous picnic area. For info and a map, call Point Reyes National Seashore at 415-663-1092.

RISEN FROM THE ASHES

If you watched TV newscasts in October 1995, you may think there's nothing left of Point Reyes. In fact, only 12,000 of the National Seashore's 68,000 acres burned in that wildfire, leaving most of the park and this entire route untouched. Even the charred acreage, in the park's north-central section, is rapidly regenerating as new vegetation and tiny bishop pines sprout from the ashes.

That was the second time in this century that the peninsula was ravaged by a natural disaster. The 1906 quake literally split open the San Andreas fault, yards from where the Visitor Center now stands. It was the most powerful quake of the century in the continental United States, and evidence of it remains on the Earthquake Trail, a .75-mile loop from the Visitor Center.

Not to worry. The odds that a quake or wildfire will ruin your run through Point Reyes are far smaller than the chances that you'll fall in love with a hiker at Arch Rock.

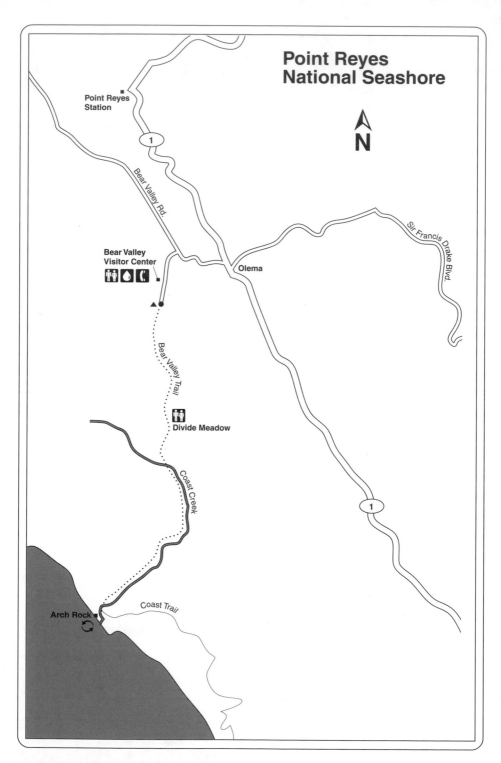

Point Reyes
National Seashore

N

Point Reyes
Station

1

Bear Valley Rd

Sir Francis Drake Blvd.

Bear Valley
Visitor Center

Olema

Bear Valley Trail

Divide Meadow

Coast Creek

1

Arch Rock

Coast Trail

ANGEL ISLAND LOOP

4.7 MILES	ROAD 🚻 💧 📞	SCENERY RATING	🏖️ 🏖️ 🏖️ 🏖️ 🏖️
		HILL RATING	⛰️ ⛰️ ⛰️ ⛰️ ⛰️

More than half the fun is getting there because 750-acre Angel Island State Park is accessible only by ferry—and inaccessible to cars. For generations, Bay Area families have ferried to this peaceful island between San Francisco and Tiburon for picnics and hikes. More recently, runners have discovered its undulating perimeter loop.

ACCESS

Take a ferry from Fisherman's Wharf in San Francisco (800-BAY CRUISE or 415-546-2628), Jack London Square in Oakland (510-522-3300), or downtown Tiburon (415-435-2131).

COURSE

Turn (L) off the ferry dock to North Ridge trailhead. Make the short, steep, trail and stair climb to paved Perimeter Rd. Run a complete loop of the island in either direction, then return down North Ridge Trail to the dock.

FOOT NOTES

As you circle the island you will pass a Civil War fort (Camp Reynolds), a 90-year-old immigration station (the Ellis Island of the West), and quiet Quarry Beach, which offers a stunning view of the San Francisco skyline. Oak, madrone, pine, eucalyptus, and cypress trees line the road.

Except for one steep, 220-yard climb halfway around the island, the persistent grades aren't so long and arduous that they prevent you from enjoying the views of the bay and its bridges. Afterward, picnic on the big lawn, visit the small museum, rent a mountain bike, or hike the rest of North Ridge Trail to the summit of Mt. Livermore—a 781 elevation-foot climb with a five-county panorama at the top. For information, call Angel Island State Park at 415-435-1915.

If you'd like to race around the island, the Angel Island Run is always on the first Saturday in May. It draws about 750 runners and walkers, and a 12:30 P.M. start lets you sleep in. Contact The Guardsmen, 120 Montgomery St., #225, San Francisco, CA 94104; 415-781-6785.

TIP

If you like crowds (and wildflowers), visit the island on a weekend in May. If you don't, visit on a winter weekend (the ferries don't operate on winter weekdays) to revel in the solitude.

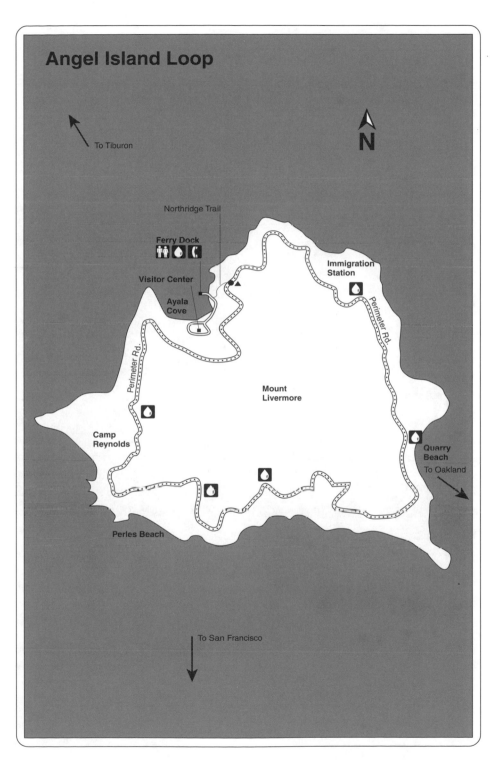

Angel Island Loop

To Tiburon

N

Northridge Trail

Ferry Dock

Visitor Center

Ayala
Cove

Immigration
Station

Perimeter Rd.

Perimeter Rd.

Mount
Livermore

Camp
Reynolds

Quarry
Beach

To Oakland

Perles Beach

To San Francisco

EAST BAY

I've run all over the world and I have never found trails as nice as those in the East Bay.
—Regina Jacobs, 1997 World Championships silver medalist, 1,500 meters

Where else in a place as densely populated as the East Bay can you find so many well-maintained parklands and trails? From the marshy baylands to the top of the Bay Area's highest peak, Mt. Diablo, more than 1,000 miles of trails, many of them interconnecting, lace Alameda and Contra Costa Counties. Most are managed by the East Bay Regional Park District (EBRPD); the several routes in this chapter on EBRPD lands represent only a taste. It's a treat to explore any of the district's 53 parks—there are trails in nearly all of them—from the Point Pinole Regional Shoreline at the northern tip of the East Bay to the Ohlone Wilderness Regional Trail in the southern corner of Alameda County.

The East Bay Municipal Utility District (EBMUD) maintains 63 miles of back-country trails. Using the trails requires a permit ($10 per year, 510-835-3000). EBMUD also oversees trails where no permit is required at Lafayette Reservoir, Lake Chabot, and the San Pablo Reservoir.

Mt. Diablo State Park (925-837-2525) boasts over 100 miles of trails. Trail runners may want to check out the "Devil Mountain," which is not included in this book because most of the trails are painfully steep and there are better options.

Whether your preference is trails, bike paths, or roads—on flat, rolling, or steep terrain—the East Bay has more to offer than you could ever imagine by driving up and down its freeways.

TRANSIT

The East Bay is served by ferries and BART trains that connect to San Francisco, as well as BART Express, AC Transit, and local bus lines. BART will transport you to within a few blocks to a few miles of most of the routes, with bus connections (or a jog) getting you the rest of the way. For timetables, call 510-817-1717.

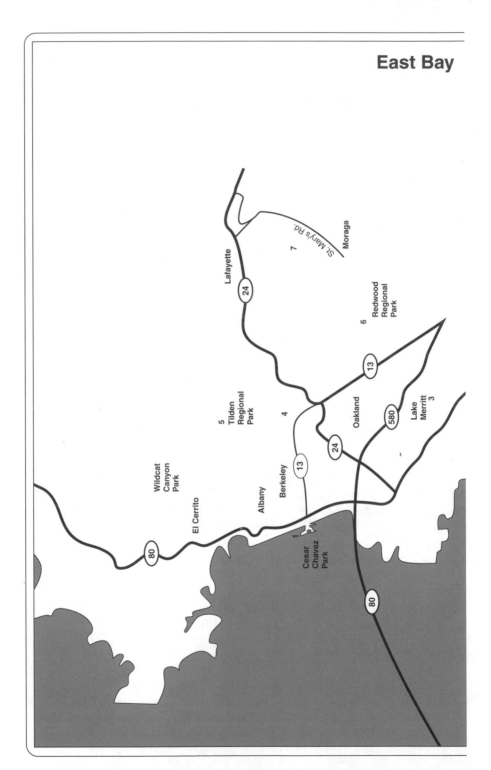

East Bay

Lafayette

St. Mary's Rd

Moraga

7

24

6

Redwood
Regional
Park

13

5
Tilden
Regional
Park

4

Oakland

580

Lake
Merritt
3

Wildcat
Canyon
Park

El Cerrito

24

13

Albany

Berkeley

13

80

1

Cesar
Chavez
Park

80

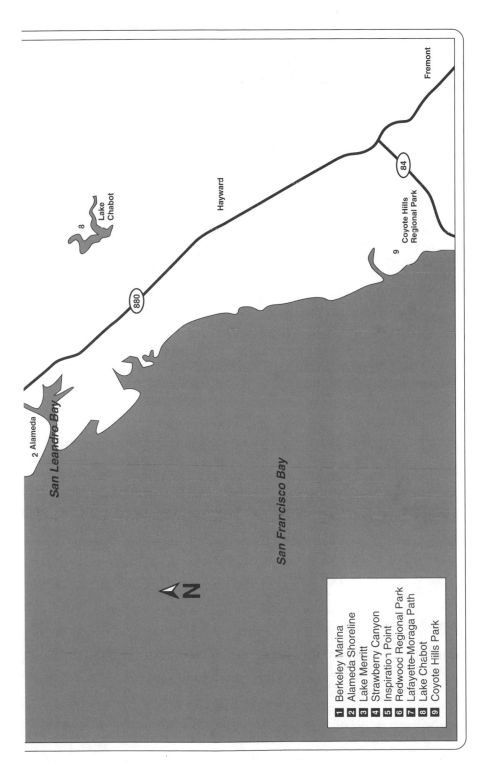

Lake Chabot

Hayward

84

Coyote Hills
Regional Park

9

880

Fremont

2 Alameda

San Leandro Bay

San Francisco Bay

N

1 Berkeley Marina
2 Alameda Shoreline
3 Lake Merritt
4 Strawberry Canyon
5 Inspiration Point
6 Redwood Regional Park
7 Lafayette-Moraga Path
8 Lake Chabot
9 Coyote Hills Park

BERKELEY MARINA

4.9 MILES	ROAD/TRAIL	SCENERY RATING	
	👥 💧 ☎	HILL RATING	

Any time that you drive past the University exit on I-80 in Berkeley, chances are you'll be traveling about your slow-day running speed. To take a break from the traffic, slip on your running clothes at the Berkeley Pier restroom and get going on this peaceful, stress-reducing run on the bay. The traffic will at least *seem* better by the time you're back on the freeway.

ACCESS

From the Bay Bridge, drive I-80-East to University Ave. exit. Take University Ave. west, (L) on Marina Blvd., (L) on Seawall Dr., and park immediately on right. Or take BART to downtown Berkeley, and AC Transit #51 bus to start.

COURSE

With one key exception, stay on course by keeping the water on your left. Run north (past the pier) along Seawall Dr. After flipping a "U" at the Berkeley Yacht Club, loop counterclockwise around the marina. Beyond the boats, turn (R) along the bay into Cesar Chavez Park. Run on the bike path, grass, or dirt trail, all of which follow the bay around three sides of this square, grassy park. Instead of following the water left toward I-80, go straight along Marina Blvd. Just after crossing University Ave., take the bike path (L) into Shorebird Park. Stay beside the bay the rest of the way to the pier. For an extra mile, go out-and-back on the concrete fishing pier.

FOOT NOTES

This route is surprisingly peaceful, with stunning views of the bay, the bridges, and the hills. It's mostly on flat bike paths, but there are dirt trails and gentle rollers in Chavez Park. That's also where you'll encounter the most runners, and where .25-mile posts mark the way. Afterward, you can spend more time watching the shorebirds from the windows of one of the restaurants you've just run past.

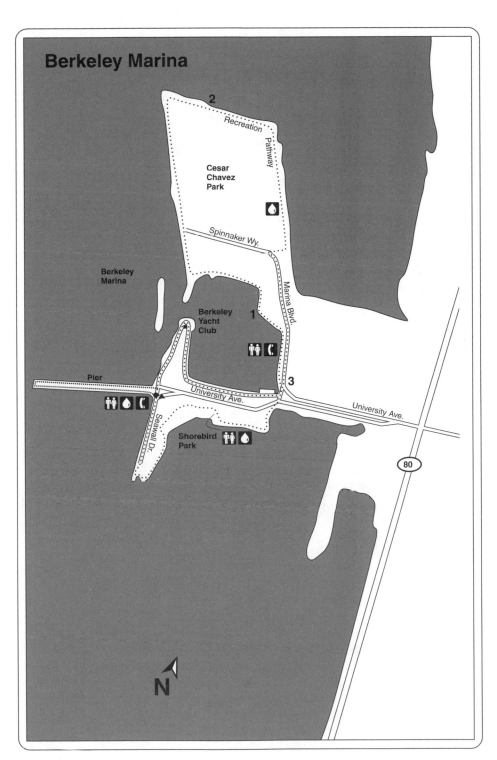

Berkeley Marina

2

Recreation Pathway

Cesar
Chavez
Park

Spinnaker Wy.

Berkeley
Marina

Marina Blvd.

Berkeley
Yacht
Club

1

3

Pier

University Ave.

University Ave.

Seawall Dr.

Shorebird
Park

80

N

ALAMEDA SHORELINE

10.8 MILES	ROAD/SAND	SCENERY RATING					
	👫 💧 ☎	HILL RATING					

Residents of Alameda have a juicy recreation secret: miles of well-groomed bike paths, dirt paths, and beaches along the bay on Alameda (an island) and across San Leandro Channel on Bay Farm Island (actually a peninsula shared by Oakland International Airport). Many local runners and walkers enjoy these baylands, which are worth the short voyage to the "islands."

ACCESS

From Oakland or San Jose, drive I-80 to 23rd Ave./Alameda exit. The flow of traffic puts you on Park St. Follow Park St. to its end, and turn (R) on Shore Line Dr., (R) on Shell Gate Rd., and park immediately. Or the Harbor Bay Ferry (510-769-5500) takes you from San Francisco's Ferry Building at the foot of Market St. to the route's 3.5-mile point.

COURSE

Cross Shore Line and turn (L) to run east along the bay bike path or on the sand of Alameda Beach. After 1.2 miles, the beach ends at a marshy bird sanctuary. Stay along the water by continuing straight on the narrow, sandy trail, which changes into pavement before reaching an auto drawbridge. Follow the bike path under that bridge, then turn (L) twice to get onto the *pedestrian* drawbridge to Bay Farm Island. At the end of the bridge, turn (R) onto another pedestrian bridge that drops you onto a bay-hugging bike path. Follow the bike path until it ends at the South Loop Rd. stoplight. Return the same way.

FOOT NOTES

The start and finish of this flat route cover the same territory as the first mile of the Run for the Parks 10K, held in August. Most of the route is on Bay Farm Island bike paths with .5-mile markers and a parallel dirt path right on the bay. You may want to shorten the route on breezy days by turning around early because the miles nearest the turnaround are the windiest. Afterward, picnic on the beach or stop for a sandwich on Park St. on the drive back to the freeway.

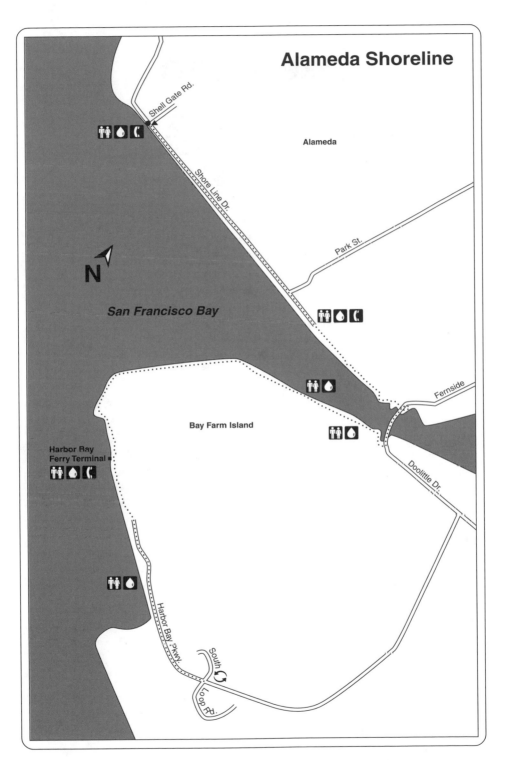

Alameda Shoreline

Shell Gate Rd.

Alameda

Shore Line Dr.

Park St.

N

San Francisco Bay

Fernside

Bay Farm Island

Harbor Bay
Ferry Terminal

Doolittle Dr.

Harbor Bay Pkwy.

South
Loop Rd.

LAKE MERRITT

The answer: Oakland's Lake Merritt.

The question: When is running in the middle of a big city *not* running in the middle of a big city? Like New York's Central Park, Lake Merritt is an oasis of footpaths and greenery with a surprising assortment of birds in the heart of Oakland. There are quieter and prettier places to run in the East Bay, but none as populated with exercisers—from casual walkers to serious racers—to make the time go by a little faster and make the effort a little easier.

ACCESS

From the Bay Bridge, drive I-580-East to Grand Ave. exit, turn (R) on Grand Ave., and proceed nine short blocks; turn (L) at the second crossing of Bellevue Ave. (a one-way street). Proceed to Sailboat House sign and park. Parking on Bellevue Ave. is free on weekdays, but costs $2 on weekends and holidays, or you can feed a meter instead. Or take BART to Lake Merritt station and jog five short blocks east on Lakeside Dr. to the 2.0-mile point of the route.

COURSE

As you proceed clockwise around the lake on paths, you'll be within 75 meters of the water for most of the way. There are no street crossings, although the path does head inland twice in the second half of the loop, once to go around the Oakland Parks Department building and once to go up the hill at Children's Fairyland.

FOOT NOTES

Most of the route is gently rolling. You have a choice of surfaces as you circle the lake, alternating between paved bike paths, narrow dirt paths, grass, concrete promenades, and a short stretch of sandy beach.

Look up to appreciate the rich variety of urban architecture that surrounds the lake, from old, ornately embellished, low-rise apartment buildings to the gleaming, high-rise office buildings. Look down and you may also notice the darker side of urban life: litter on the ground and in the lake. Park maintenance crews, however, do a decent job of keeping the area clean and bicycling cops keep it reasonably safe.

A refreshing aspect of the route is the runners who circle the lake and wave to each other in passing. They form a community of sorts in the middle of a city not well-known for its hospitality.

If you like the lake, you'll want to try Oakland's largest race, the Valentine Day Run/Walk. The 5K and 10K races (one loop or two) draw thousands of competitors on the second Sunday of February. For information, contact the American Heart Association, 11200 Golf Links Rd., Oakland, CA 94605, 510-632-9606.

LAKE OF THE PEOPLE

"There are always people walking and running around Lake Merritt," says Oakland's Regina Jacobs, "and that helps to keep me going on days when I don't feel that much like running. It's also pretty flat, so it's a good place for fast tempo runs as well as easy recovery runs."

Regina, a Stanford graduate, has been the most accomplished 1,500-meter runner in America for a decade, with berths on the 1988, 1992, and 1996 Olympic teams. She placed 10th in the 1996 Olympic 1,500-meter final and won the silver medal in the 1997 World Championships 1,500 meters. She runs around the lake often. "I've even run around it with a friend at night," she notes. A string of lights between antique lampposts illuminates the lake's paths, making night running possible—but don't do it alone.

TIP

If you wear a heart-rate monitor, as Regina Jacobs often does during her loops around Lake Merritt, keep in mind that electrical interference can send the read-outs into orbit. "If your monitor suddenly shows a heart-rate of 250," she advises, "don't worry. It isn't a heart attack."

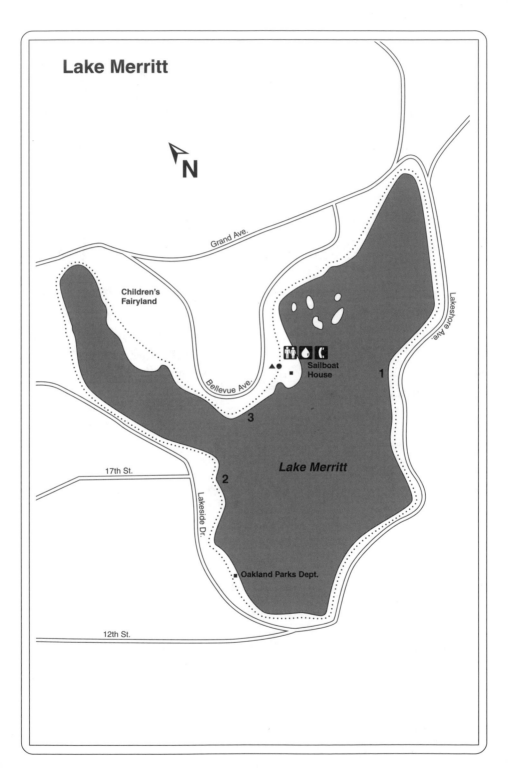

Lake Merritt

N

Grand Ave.

Children's
Fairyland

Lakeshore Ave.

Sailboat
House

Bellevue Ave.

1

3

Lake Merritt

17th St.

2

Lakeside Dr.

Oakland Parks Dept.

12th St.

STRAWBERRY CANYON

7.5 MILES	TRAIL ☎	SCENERY RATING	(4 of 5 mountains)
		HILL RATING	(3 of 5 hills)

This botanically rich route is within the University of California-Berkeley Ecological Study Area.

ACCESS

From the Bay Bridge, take I-80-East. Exit onto University Ave. and drive 2.0 miles. Turn (L) on Oxford St. for two blocks; turn (R) on Hearst Ave. for .5 mile to another (R) turn onto Gayley Rd. Go .3 mile and turn (L) at Haas Clubhouse & Pools sign (Stadium Rimway). After .2 mile turn (L) on Centennial Dr. and proceed .7 mile to the first parking lot on the right, past the swimming pools. If the lot's 10 spaces are taken, drive back to the Haas Clubhouse Pool lot, which adds .3 mile each way to the running distance on an uphill gravel path along Centennial Dr. Or take BART to downtown Berkeley, hop a UCB Shuttle bus to Memorial Stadium, and jog .7 mile up Centennial Dr. to the start.

COURSE

Wooden stairs from the 10-space parking lot lead to a smooth, dirt fire road that you will follow the entire way. Just before the fire road reaches a residential street at .9 mile, veer (L) up a short, steep stretch. Ignore the two fire roads that come in from the right in the second mile. Partway up a short, steep climb in the fourth mile, the road splits. Take the right fork, which soon ends at Grizzly Peak Blvd. Head back.

FOOT NOTES

After a steadily and moderately climbing first mile under a thick canopy of leaf and needle trees, the course is gradually uphill and flat the rest of the way to the turnaround. You will follow a counter-clockwise semicircular cut in the canyon. Visible below are university research buildings, the main campus, and beyond it, the city of Berkeley, the bay, and the Golden Gate Bridge.

If you want to run farther, at the turnaround point go (L) on Grizzly Peak Blvd. for 300 meters, then (R) into Tilden Regional Park. From there you can explore hilly trails as much as you wish before making the downhill return trip through Strawberry Canyon. For a Tilden Regional Park trail map, call 510-635-0135.

Afterward, stop by one of the many off-campus coffeehouses, where instead of fomenting revolution they're busy foaming cappuccinos.

MR. POWERBAR'S CANYON

Brian Maxwell says that running the Strawberry Canyon trail three times a week in the 1970s turned him into a marathoner. "Because the top of the trail is at the Tilden Park gate, I often added a few miles on Tilden's trails before running back down," he recalls. "Those long runs drew me into racing longer."

The result was a trio of 2:14 marathons and victories at a dozen major marathons, including the 1980 Canadian Olympic Trials. Still, mixed among those successes were some failures caused by stomach distress, a problem that Brian solved in his kitchen when he concocted the first PowerBar. He is now president and CEO of PowerFoods, the company that dominates the product category it created, and through it all, he's remained a Strawberry faithful.

"The trail very quickly transports you from an urban environment to a very natural setting. There are spots where you can imagine you're in the Sierras, and then at the top is that spectacular view."

Brian also has praise for the varying terrain, from flat to viciously steep. "When I coached the U.C. cross-country team [1975-1983], I had them run hard on various parts of the trail. But the best story I've heard about Strawberry is that John Walker, on an extended visit to Berkeley, did repeat sprints up the 'connector' [the steep, 200-meter grade at the 1.0-mile point] shortly before he broke the world record in the mile."

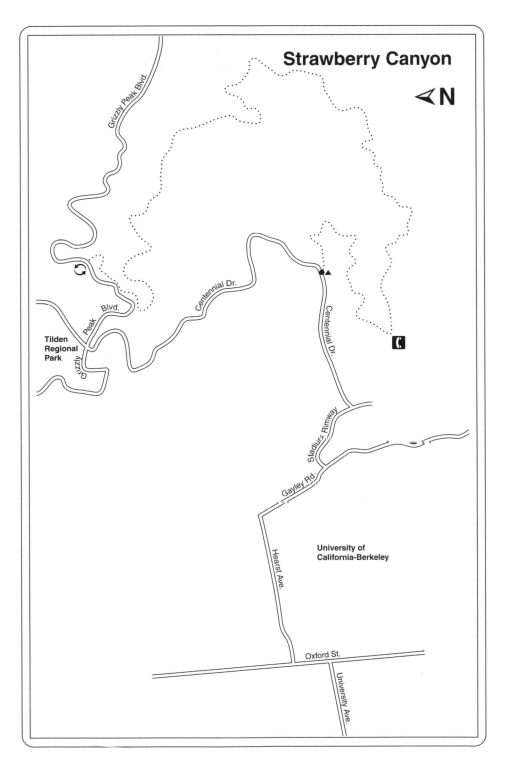

Strawberry Canyon

N

Grizzly Peak Blvd.

Centennial Dr.

Peak   Blvd.

Grizzly

Tilden
Regional
Park

Centennial Dr.

Stadium Rimway

Gayley Rd.

University of
California-Berkeley

Hearst Ave.

Oxford St.

University Ave.

INSPIRATION POINT

7.2 MILES	ROAD/TRAIL	SCENERY RATING	
	👫	HILL RATING	

Inspiration Point is aptly named. It provides views of San Pablo Reservoir and San Pablo Bay at a distance, and the forests and grassy hillsides of Tilden and Wildcat Canyon Regional Parks in the foreground. You're treated to this view for most of the run on the narrow, hilly, 1,000-foot-high spine of the hills above Albany and El Cerrito.

ACCESS

From the Bay Bridge, take I-80-East to the Albany exit. Go east on Buchanan St. for .6 mile, then turn (R) on Marin Ave. where the road splits. After a steep climb, turn (R) on Grizzly Peak Blvd. for .9 mile, then turn (L) on Shasta Rd. into Tilden Regional Park. Do not take the golf course road, but continue straight onto Wildcat Canyon Rd. and follow signs to the Inspiration Point lot on the left. There is no public transit.

COURSE

Next to the parking lot is the trailhead. "Nimitz Way" is carved into stone pillars. Follow this bike path, or the dirt shoulder that parallels it, to Havey Canyon Trail. (One way to know you're there is that going any farther means climbing a long, steep hill.) Head back the same way.

FOOT NOTES

Alongside hikers, mountain bikers, and equestrians, you'll pass through redwood and eucalyptus groves, but most of the course is an unshaded ridge and is at the mercy of the elements. You're also at the mercy of hills—ups and downs in the first and last quarters, a long descent in the second quarter, and then back up it in the third quarter.

Ambitious? You can add on many hilly miles on Tilden and Wildcat Canyon Regional Parks' interconnecting trails (call 510-635-0135 for free maps), some of which branch off Nimitz. A perfect summertime post-run treat is a swim in Tilden Regional Park's Lake Anza.

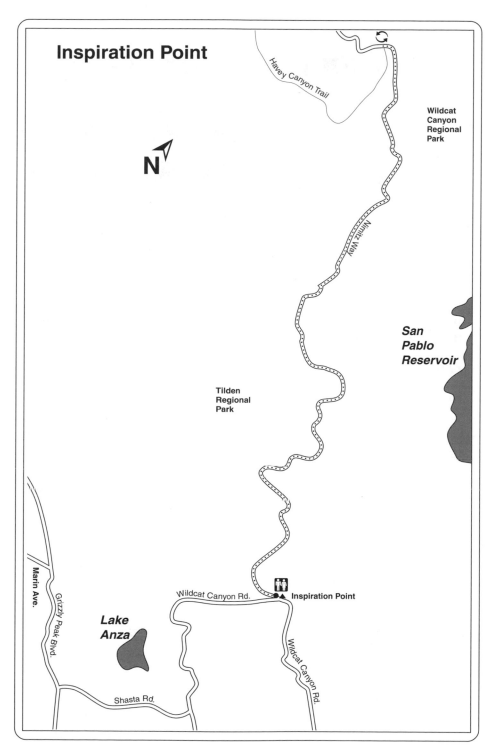

Inspiration Point

Havey Canyon Trail

Wildcat
Canyon
Regional
Park

N

Nimitz Way

San
Pablo
Reservoir

Tilden
Regional
Park

Marin Ave.

Grizzly Peak Blvd.

Wildcat Canyon Rd.

Inspiration Point

Lake
Anza

Wildcat Canyon Rd.

Shasta Rd.

REDWOOD REGIONAL PARK

8.0 MILES	TRAIL	SCENERY RATING	
		HILL RATING	

Attempt this Oakland hills route only when you're well-rested; the roller-coaster hills are relentless. What makes it worth the suffering, however, are the training value and the variety. Running it even occasionally will get you into great shape. As for the variety, the trail is constantly changing from narrow to wide, sunny to shady, and powdery dirt to rocky, unforgiving earth. You progress from groves of towering redwoods to low brush, and from gently rolling hills to steep pitches that make your teeth ache.

ACCESS

From the Bay Bridge, drive I-580-East, Hwy. 24-East, and Hwy. 13-South to Park Blvd. exit. Turn (L) on Park Blvd., (L) on Mountain Blvd., go two blocks and turn (R) onto Snake Rd. for two blocks. Go straight at Shepherd Canyon, turn (R) on Skyline Blvd. for .4 mile to the Skyline Gate lot on the left. No public transit.

COURSE

Main route. From the parking lot, take West Ridge Trail. Like all of the park's trails, it is well-marked, but there is one unmarked fork just past the archery range (1.8 miles). Take the left fork. When West Ridge Trail ends (4.4 miles) at the bottom of a long, steep descent at Bridle Trail, turn (L) for 350 meters, and then (R) at the To Canyon Meadow sign. This path crosses a gully to a grass field. Run to the top of the field to Canyon Trail. Canyon Trail brings you up to East Ridge Trail; turn (L) and proceed 2.9 miles to the finish.

Alternate route (7.5 miles). Follow the main route to the grass field, then turn (L) on Stream Trail, a wide dirt road. This is a shorter and easier return trip through picnic areas and redwood groves.

FOOT NOTES

You'll face steep hills and long hills, but the only long *and* steep hills are almost back-to-back in the fifth mile—a .5-mile descent to the end of West Ridge Trail and a .5-mile climb up Canyon Trail. The latter is so steep you may want to powerwalk it.

You're rewarded for the effort with views of Oakland from West Ridge and Mt. Diablo from East Ridge. Both trails are packed on weekends with runners, mountain bikers, equestrians, and walkers.

If you wish to shorten or lengthen your outing, there are many trails that branch off of West Ridge and East Ridge. Most are narrow and hilly. You can get a trail map from EBRPD Publications, 510-635-0135.

HILLS OF THE STARS

Redwood Park is a favorite venue for many East Bay runners, including 1996 U.S. Olympic marathoner Linda Somers and masters star Shirley Matson.

"The East Ridge–West Ridge trail loop is a great workout," says Somers, "because it's got some tough hills. But the trail conditions are quite good, so you can open up if you're feeling good. And the views are great."

Matson, who holds most of the U.S. age 50–54 and age 55–59 records, runs the Redwood Park trails three times a week. "I'd run them every day, but all the upsies-downsies means you have to give yourself recovery days," she says. "It's well worth it, though, for the serenity and the scenery."

Both women note that with the interconnecting trails you can design many loops within the park and, for runs longer than 10 miles, you can devise loops that venture south into Chabot Regional Park. In Redwood Park, Somers says that she likes to vary her route by adding narrow and rugged French Trail; Matson favors Stream Trail. Both run the length of the park, between and parallel to West Ridge and East Ridge.

TIP

If you run any of the narrow trails off of either route, wear high socks, especially in the fall. Poison oak is everywhere!

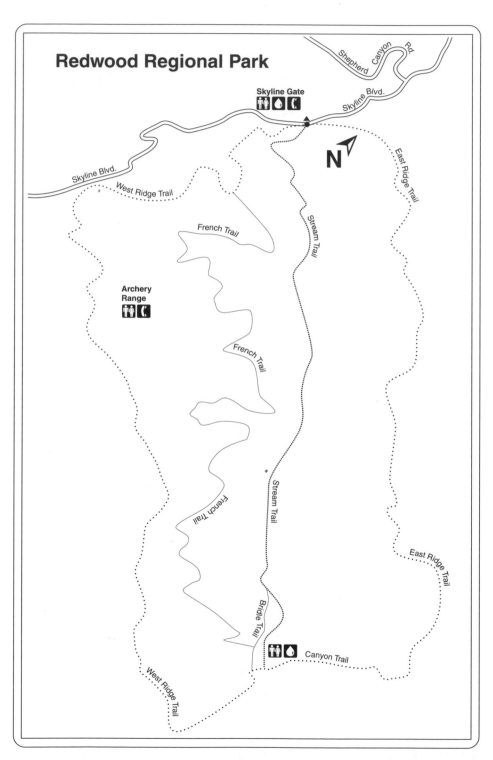

Redwood Regional Park

Skyline Gate

Archery Range

West Ridge Trail

French Trail

French Trail

French Trail

Stream Trail

Stream Trail

Bridle Trail

Canyon Trail

East Ridge Trail

East Ridge Trail

Skyline Blvd.

Skyline Blvd.

Shepherd Canyon Rd.

West Ridge Trail

N

LAFAYETTE-MORAGA PATH

11.3 MILES	ROAD/TRAIL	SCENERY RATING					
		HILL RATING					

How can you beat an out-and-back course where the "out" seems pretty flat and the "back" is decidedly downhill most of the way? Don't argue the physics, just enjoy the scenery alongside shaded Las Trampas Creek, which often plunges below the path into deep gorges.

ACCESS

From Oakland, I-580-East, Hwy. 24-East to the Pleasant Hill Rd. exit (Lafayette). Turn (R) on Pleasant Hill Rd. for .9 mile to its end. Turn (R) on Olympic Blvd. for .2 mile, and turn (R) on Reliez Station Rd. Take an immediate (R) into the parking lot. If the six parking spaces are taken, drive back to the first lot you passed on Olympic and run the extra .2 mile. Or take BART to Lafayette, County Connection #206 bus to Pleasant Hill/Olympic.

COURSE

Just across Reliez Station Rd. at the crosswalk is the beginning of the Lafayette-Moraga Regional Trail. The only turn on the route is between 2.75 and 3.00 miles (painted on the asphalt), where you need to cross St. Mary's Road instead of taking the path alongside the road. Turning around at the crossing gives you a fairly level 5.8-mile run. Longer options include turning back at Moraga Commons (shortly beyond the "5.50" marker at the restrooms) for this 11.3-miler, or at the end of the bike path for a whopping 14.5-mile roundtrip. Markings every .25 mile and every kilometer let you turn around anywhere without having to guess at the distance.

FOOT NOTES

This course is full of paradoxes. First is the 400-foot elevation gain to the turnaround, which you hardly notice because most of it is so subtly graded. The only noticeable climb (followed by a moderate descent to the turnaround) steepens to a crest across from 135-year-old St. Mary's College at 4.6 miles, but even at its steepest it's nothing to fret over.

Another paradox is the rural feel to the bike-path route. Much of the course lies within a mile of Hwy. 24, but it seems that you're in ranch country rather than between the backyards of ranch-style homes. The route crosses many streets, but most have so little traffic that you probably won't have to stop for motorists. The wooded middle miles are particularly tranquil. A dirt shoulder lets you tread lightly and exercise stations at both ends of the route are another plus. For info and a map, call EBRPD at 510-635-0135.

RAILS TO TRAILS

The Lafayette-Moraga bike path is a shining triumph of the "rails-to-trails" movement. Soon after its conversion in 1992, the path was drawing an estimated 500,000 annual users—runners, walkers, cyclists, skaters, and equestrians. Not bad for an abandoned rail corridor.

Also called "linear parks" or "rail-trails," these land-use conversions capitalize on the trends away from rail commerce and toward outdoor fitness. More than 1,000 rail-trails in 45 states are completed or underway, including many in the Bay Area. Among them are the Sir Francis Drake Bikeway that parallels Corte Madera Creek in central Marin; the Mill Valley-to-Sausalito Bike Path through tidal marshlands; the Ohlone Greenway that runs beneath BART tracks from El Cerrito to Berkeley; and the Lands End (San Francisco) trail described in chapter 1.

New projects and extensions of existing rail-trails are in progress throughout the Bay Area. If you would like to get behind this effort, contact the local chapter of the 70,000-member Rails-to-Trails Conservancy, 415-397-2220.

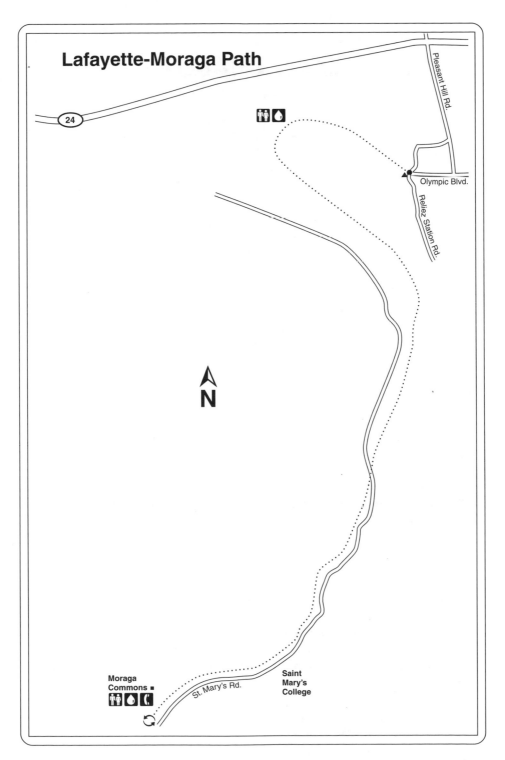

Lafayette-Moraga Path

24

🚻💧

Olympic Blvd.

Pleasant Hill Rd.

Relliez Station Rd.

N

Moraga
Commons ■
🚻💧🔋

St. Mary's Rd.

Saint
Mary's
College

LAKE CHABOT

6.2 MILES	ROAD/TRAIL 👥 💧 ☎	SCENERY RATING	🌳🌳🌳🌳
		HILL RATING	

Lake Chabot is a gem: 2.0 miles off the freeway, but many miles away in mood. Steep hills cradle the 315-acre reservoir, keeping most of the sights of nearby civilization hidden from view. This allows runners, fishermen, and other outdoor addicts to really unwind. This route wanders from cove to cove as it traces the eastern arm of the lake.

ACCESS

From Oakland, I-580-East to Fairmont Dr. exit (San Leandro). Turn (L) on Fairmont Dr. and go 2.0 miles to Lake Chabot Marina sign. U-turn and park outside the park entrance to duck a $3 fee. No public transit.

COURSE

Walk past the entrance gate to a display board where the bike path forks. Run down the right fork (an unnamed trail). You'll pass the Turtle and Willow picnic areas before heading counterclockwise around the lake on the East Shore Trail. About .1 mile past the end of the paved bike path (2.0 miles), turn (L) over the long footbridge (Bicycle Loop sign). Just beyond the bridge, turn (L) again on Honker Bay Trail. After 1.0 mile, turn around at the foot of a steep climb (there's a small fishing pier and outhouse). Return.

FOOT NOTES

The first and last quarters of the route are undulating, but with no long or steep rises. Quarter miles are painted on the paved bike-path portion, which offers a dirt shoulder. The quiet middle section (Honker Bay Trail) is mostly flat on a wide, dirt, lake-hugging path.

If you wish to run farther and tackle some hills, the trails that venture away from the lakeshore are a trail runner's paradise. The adventurous may want to circle the lake on the Half Marathon Loop, a patchwork of trails shown on the display map at the start of the trail. Info: Lake Chabot Regional Park, 510-582-2198.

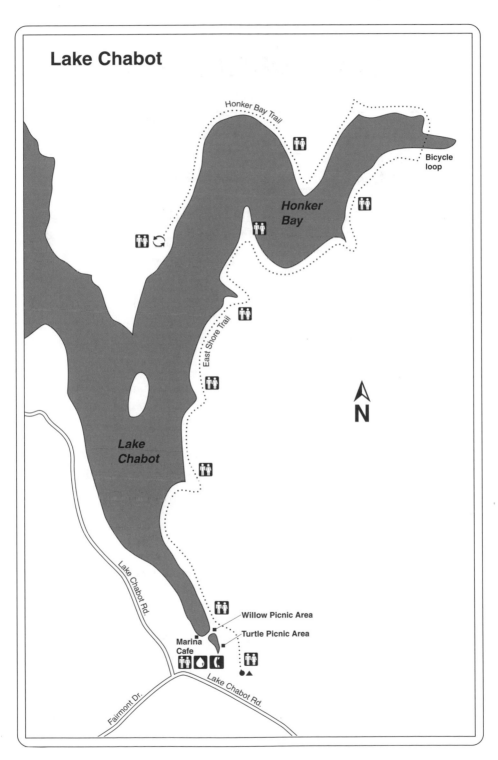

Lake Chabot

Honker Bay Trail

Bicycle loop

Honker Bay

East Shore Trail

Lake Chabot

N

Lake Chabot Rd.

Willow Picnic Area

Turtle Picnic Area

Marina Cafe

Lake Chabot Rd.

Fairmont Dr.

COYOTE HILLS PARK

The trails in and around Coyote Hills Regional Park are an excellent place to explore the biodiversity of the baylands. Most of this route is alongside marshlands or the bay's salt ponds.

ACCESS

From Oakland, take I-880-South, then I-84-West (Fremont) for two exits to Paseo Padre Pkwy. Turn (R) on Paseo Padre Pkwy. for 1.1 miles; then (L) on Patterson Ranch Rd. for 1.4 miles to the Visitor Center. No public transit.

COURSE

At trailhead near parking lot entrance, take Chochenyo Trail into the marsh. Go straight on D.U.S.T. Trail (.4 mile), (L) on Alameda Creek Trail (1.2 miles), and (L) at the gravel road (Pelican Trail) marked only by a post showing a hiker (3.1 miles). This becomes a narrow levee path, surrounded by water, which ends at a paved bike path (Bayview Trail, 4.1 miles). Turn (R) and follow Bayview Trail along the bay, then inland to Patterson Ranch Rd. Just across the road, turn (L) on the bike path, which leads back to the Visitor Center.

FOOT NOTES

This route, with its traffic-free dirt and gravel roads, trails, and paved bike paths, starts with a tour of a restored wetland infested by ducks, quail, and five-foot-tall herons that stand right on the trail. In the second half, there are a few short, mild hills, and views of the bay and two bridges.

The route is a great launching point for longer runs on traffic-free levees. You can add up to 18 miles out-and-back by turning (R) instead of (L) on the Alameda Creek Regional Trail. The Alameda Creek Trail (paved on the north side of the wide creek, dirt on the south side) extends all the way to Fremont's Niles district. Adventurous types can explore the endless levee paths that frame the bay's salt ponds west of the park, which are part of the San Francisco Bay National Wildlife Refuge.

Afterward, stop by the Visitor Center or picnic on the lawn. The park is open 8:00 A.M. to 6:00 P.M. For information and a map, call 510-795-9385.

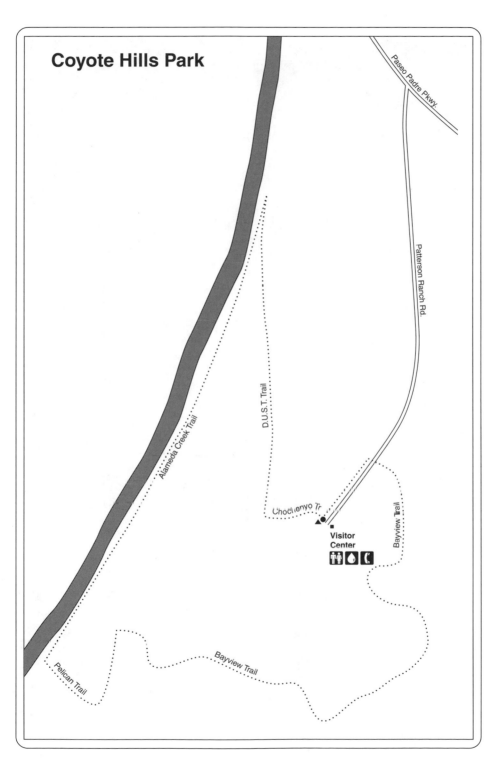

Coyote Hills Park

Paseo Padre Pkwy.

Patterson Ranch Rd.

Alameda Creek Trail

D.U.S.T. Trail

Chochenyo Tr.

Bayview Trail

Visitor
Center

Bayview Trail

Pelican Trail

SOUTH BAY

It's beautiful here. The variety of terrain, the mild climate, and the quality and sheer number of trails combine to make it one of the best places in the world to run.

—Nancy Ditz, first U.S. finisher, 1988 Olympic Marathon

Nancy has spent all her life in the South Bay. She grew up in Los Altos Hills, graduated from Stanford University, and moved to Menlo Park and Woodside while her talent as a road racer and marathoner emerged. She won most of the major Bay Area races in the 1980s so something about training in the South Bay must have worked for her—as it did for fellow Olympic runners like Matt Giusto, PattiSue Plumer, and Jeff Atkinson.

For the purposes of this book, I define the South Bay as the two counties immediately south of San Francisco: San Mateo and Santa Clara, which extend to San Jose and beyond. While growing up in Redwood City, I came to appreciate South Bay running by exploring the trails above Woodside and the country roads near Stanford. There are flats near the bay and on the narrow plateau bisected by I-280, but also plenty of hills in the many suburbs south of San Francisco and on the forested ridge that shields these towns and cities from coastal fog and winds.

Like the rest of the Bay Area, the South Bay's parklands offer hundreds of miles of trails in San Mateo and Santa Clara County parks, and hundreds more on Mid-Peninsula Open Space District lands. The ambiance ranges from urban creeks and marshy baylands to coastal redwood groves and sprawling reservoirs.

This chapter merely skims the surface. I didn't even include the two largest parks in the South Bay because both are a bit off the beaten path:

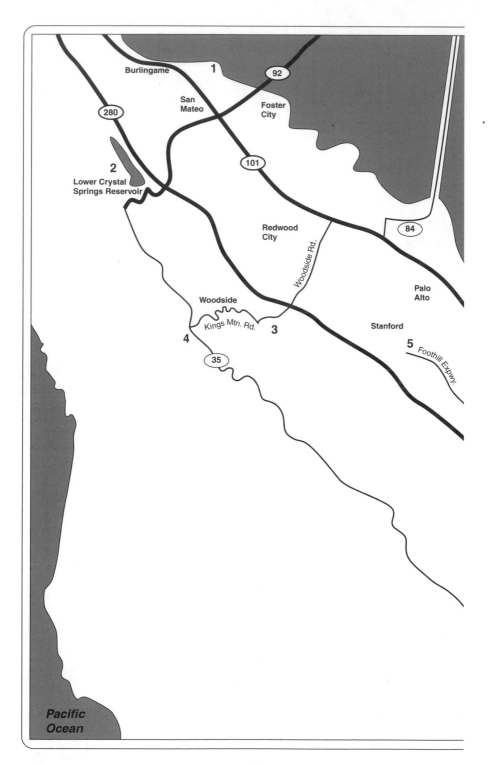

Burlingame

San
Mateo

Foster
City

280

101

1

92

2

Lower Crystal
Springs Reservoir

Redwood
City

Woodside Rd.

84

Palo
Alto

Woodside

Kings Mtn. Rd.

3

Stanford

4

5

Foothill Expwy.

35

Pacific
Ocean

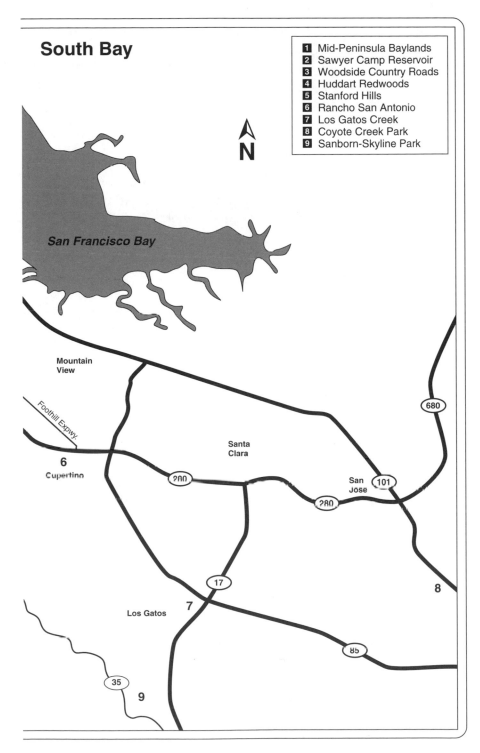

South Bay

N

San Francisco Bay

Mountain
View

Foothill Expwy.

6

Cupertino

Santa
Clara

280

San
Jose

101

280

680

17

7

Los Gatos

8

85

35

9

7,400-acre Pescadero Creek County Park near La Honda, and 9,500-acre Grant Park near Mt. Hamilton. Nor did I cover any of the marvelous running hotspots in Santa Cruz County. Nonetheless, I am certain you'll thoroughly enjoy this highly accessible collection of routes, which are all within minutes of the freeways.

TRANSIT

CalTrain connects San Francisco and San Jose, SamTrans buses cover San Mateo County and SCVTA light-rail and buses serve Santa Clara County. Unfortunately, most of them stick to the flatlands and most of these routes are in the hills. For transit timetables, call 408-817-1717.

MID-PENINSULA BAYLANDS

11.7 MILES	ROAD/TRAIL 🚻 💧 📞	SCENERY RATING	
		HILL RATING	

Any time you fly into San Francisco International Airport and sit on the left side of the plane, you can see the bay levee bike path that snakes along the shoreline of Foster City and San Mateo far below. It looks peaceful down there and it is. While running the levees you hardly hear the jets, even when they seem close enough to touch. This level bike-path course on the bay offers a dirt shoulder, proximity to freeways without freeway noise, no street crossings, and the convenience of distance markers every .25 mile, .5 mile, and mile.

ACCESS

From San Francisco, take Hwy. 101-South to Poplar Ave. exit (San Mateo). Follow "Coyote Pt." signs (two right turns), and go under freeway to the first (L) on Airport Blvd. Where Airport Blvd. bends to the right at a business park, park on the bay, at the start of the bike path. Parking here instead of at Coyote Point saves you a $4 parking tab.

From the big airport hotels, jog south on Airport Blvd. to the start. The start is an eight-minute cab ride from the airport, in case you have a layover between flights.

By public transit, take CalTrain to San Mateo station and jog 1.0 mile east on Third Ave. to the third mile of the course.

COURSE

Main route. Follow the paved bike path south through Coyote Park (ignore the gravel road to the left) to the first street crossing (Coyote Pt. Dr.). Without crossing, turn (L) onto the bike lane and follow it while keeping the golf course on your right through the park. The bike lane soon becomes a bike path that climbs onto a bay levee after leaving the park's roads. Follow the bike path along the bay until it crosses beneath the San Mateo–Hayward Bridge. Head back 50 meters past the bridge at the restrooms and fountain.

Alternate route (18.1 miles). Continue south on the bike path 3.2 miles to a small grassy park where there are restrooms, two drinking fountains, two tennis courts, and a small playground. Stretch out and head back to complete a good marathon training run.

FOOT NOTES

Other than .5 mile of rolling hills in a eucalyptus grove near the start and finish, the course is flat and unprotected from the wind. Go elsewhere on windy days unless you want a resistance workout.

Along the course you will cross two lagoons via pedestrian bridges, pass windsurfing beaches with flocks of shorebirds, and enjoy views of the bay. On the long course, you'll tour the marshlands and salt flats of Belmont Slough Wildlife Refuge. The long course takes you all the way from the San Mateo–Burlingame border to the Foster City–Redwood Shores border.

Afterward you can visit Coyote Point's seafood restaurant, nature museum, or beaches. For information, call Coyote Point Recreation Area, 650-573-2592.

GIUSTO: LEVEES TO OLYMPICS

Matt Giusto lived in Foster City when he started running as a high school freshman in 1980. All through high school he ran these bay levees. As a senior, he won the U.S. high school cross-country title. The 1996 U.S. Olympian at 5,000 meters now lives in Albuquerque, but fondly recalls his training runs on this route.

"Back then I had to climb over rocks and shells on portions of the levee and all the trails were dirt, but now it's a real nice bike path. It can get windy but that just gives you a better workout, and on clear days you can see all over the Bay Area."

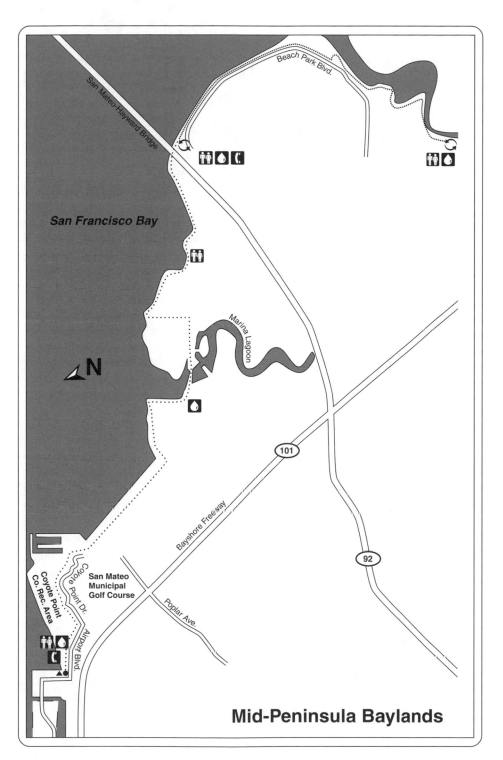

San Francisco Bay

San Mateo-Hayward Bridge

Beach Park Blvd.

Marina Lagoon

N

101

92

Bayshore Freeway

Coyote Point Dr.

Coyote Point
Co. Rec. Area

San Mateo
Municipal
Golf Course

Airport Blvd.

Poplar Ave.

Mid-Peninsula Baylands

SAWYER CAMP RESERVOIR

7.0 MILES	ROAD/TRAIL	SCENERY RATING	
	👫 💧 ☎	HILL RATING	

Just 20 minutes from San Francisco, the Sawyer Camp multi-use path is *the* place to run on the northern peninsula. The people-watching course is crowded with walkers, casual cyclists, and runners even on weekdays.

ACCESS

From San Francisco or San Jose, Hwy. 101 to Hwy. 92-West; take I-280-North for 1.3 miles to Bunker Hill Dr. exit (San Mateo). Take first (L) to cross over freeway, and then first (R) on Skyline Blvd. for .6 mile to the trailhead at Crystal Springs Rd. Park on Skyline or Crystal Springs. No public transit.

COURSE

Main Route. Follow the trail north to the 3.5-mile post, where there are restrooms and water, and return for a generally flat 7.0 miles.

Alternate Route (12 miles). To add hills and distance, continue to the end of the paved path at the 6.0-mile post (Hillcrest Blvd.).

FOOT NOTES

This course is a pleasant mix of straightaways and snaking curves; sun and shadows as you duck in and out of the shade of oak and laurel trees; and a choice of asphalt and the hard-packed-dirt-and-gravel shoulder of the bike path.

The easy main route overlooks Lower Crystal Springs Reservoir, while the 12-miler tackles a gradual to moderate 1.6-mile climb through the trees. It crests at a 130-year-old dam over San Andreas Lake. After you catch your breath on the dam, you'll confront a final, vicious, .5-mile ascent. Then jog down the other side for the last .1 mile to the turnaround. For information and a map, call San Mateo County Parks at 650-363-4020 or 650-589-5708.

TIP

On the main route, use the accurate .5-mile posts for speed training.

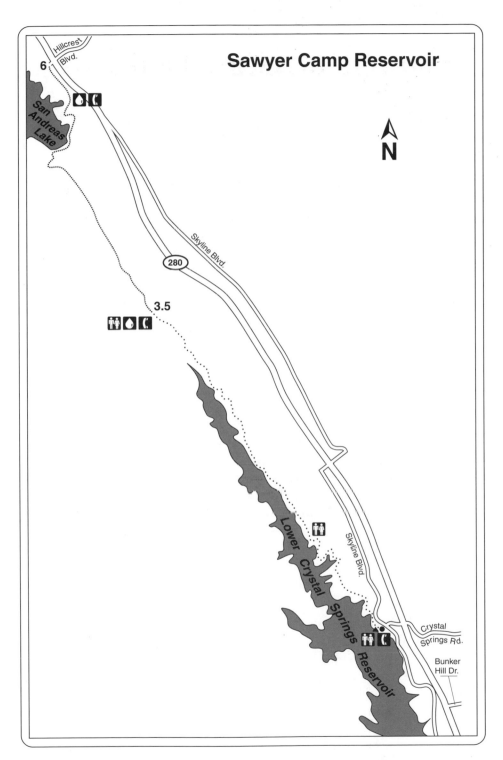

Sawyer Camp Reservoir

Hillcrest Blvd.

6

San Andreas Lake

Skyline Blvd.

280

3.5

N

Lower Crystal Springs Reservoir

Skyline Blvd.

Crystal Springs Rd.

Bunker Hill Dr.

WOODSIDE COUNTRY ROADS

In my teens, I surely logged 1,500 miles on Woodside country roads and never grew tired of them. And that wasn't behind a steering wheel. A canopy of trees creates tunnels of shelter that are almost impenetrable by winter rains and summer heat.

ACCESS

From San Francisco or San Jose, take I-280 to Woodside Rd. exit, west .8 mile on Woodside Rd. Turn (R) on Cañada Rd. for .2 mile and park across from the stone mansion. No public transit.

COURSE

Run back on Cañada Rd. to the intersection of Woodside Rd. in downtown Woodside (.2 mile). Go straight across the intersection to the wooden bridge and begin running along unmarked Mountain Home Rd. Make a sharp (R) at Portola Rd. (2.2 miles), keep straight where Portola Rd. merges with Woodside Rd. (2.8 miles), and straight again onto unmarked Tripp Rd. (Huddart Park sign) where Woodside Rd. bends to the right (3.5 miles). At the end of Tripp Rd., turn (R) on Kings Mountain Rd. (4.4 miles). At the end of Kings Mountain Rd., turn (L) on Woodside Rd. (5.1 miles), then (L) on Cañada Rd. (5.8 miles) to your car.

FOOT NOTES

This may be horse country, but you don't need four legs to enjoy prancing on the bridle trails that parallel most of these semi-rural roads. You'll also appreciate the lack of auto traffic, except for the two stretches of Woodside Rd.—and on the second stretch, there is a path separated from the road by logs.

Two landmarks are the Woodside Store (erected in 1854 and now a museum) at the intersection of Tripp and Kings Mountain Rd., and Roberts Market in downtown Woodside (the gathering spot for townies). Impressive estates at the end of long and winding driveways are barely visible from the road, owing to brick pillars and stone walls. Woodside is fragrant with old money, as green as the towering evergreens that shade your way around the course.

To add a few trail miles, enter Wunderlich County Park on Woodside Rd. at 3.3 miles.

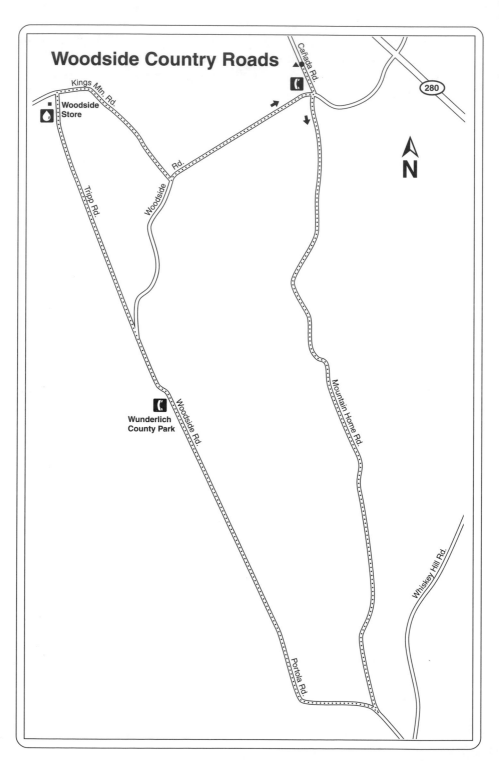

Woodside Country Roads

Cañada Rd.

280

Kings Mtn. Rd.

Woodside Store

N

Woodside Rd.

Tripp Rd.

Woodside Rd.

Wunderlich County Park

Mountain Home Rd.

Whiskey Hill Rd.

Portola Rd.

HUDDART REDWOODS

| 10.5 MILES | TRAIL 👫 💧 📞 | SCENERY RATING | |
| HILL RATING | |

Many peninsula runners have sampled the hilly trails of Huddart and Wunderlich County Parks in Woodside—and gone home exhausted. Yet the least taxing and prettiest trail in the area is the Skyline Trail, which connects the two parks at their western boundaries just below 2,000-foot Cahill Ridge. The starting point is a mere 12-minute drive off I-280.

ACCESS

From San Francisco or San Jose, take I-280 to Hwy. 92-West (San Mateo); then Hwy. 35-South (Skyline Blvd.) for 7 miles to a 10-car lot on the right (just past the 50 MPH sign). No public transit.

COURSE

Cross the road and walk 50 meters south to the trailhead (Huddart County Park sign). After 20 meters, go (R) on Skyline Trail. At .2 mile, stay (R) on Skyline Trail. Where it crosses Kings Mountain Rd. (the only road crossing), Skyline Trail narrows from a fire road into a horse trail. Head back at the 5 Mile post, because just beyond it lies a long, body-hammering descent into Wunderlich County Park.

FOOT NOTES

The trees make this course special, providing not only protection from the weather, but also a spongy carpet of pine needles and leaves on most of the path. Unfortunately, that's not all that's on the trail. Street runners should pay attention on stretches where rocks and roots are hidden under the leaves and powdery dirt. Experienced trail runners, however, will consider the Skyline an expressway as it winds through the redwoods. The Skyline Trail parallels Hwy. 35, but only once are you close enough to hear the auto traffic and only once does it cross a road.

The ridge-hugging trail is moderately undulating. Oh, you'll get a great workout—it's a good tune-up for a half marathon—but there aren't any long or steep grades. The course is well-marked, although the inaccurate mile posts are more than a mile apart. A bonus is the absence of mountain bikes; unlike many trails, you don't have to worry about colliding with a fat-tire maniac around each turn.

For endless (but hillier) variations, you can (1) head west from the start into Purisima Creek Redwoods Open Space Preserve (maps of its 21 miles of trails are at the parking lot); (2) run east into Huddart County Park by taking the Crystal Springs or Chinquapin Trail in the first .25 mile of the route; or (3) continue beyond the turnaround of this route to explore Wunderlich Park's network of trails. For Huddart and Wunderlich information and maps, call 650-363-4020.

RAT AND NANCY'S TRAIL

The ever-changing surface of the Skyline Trail, with its leaves, roots, powdery dirt (in the summer), and mud (in the winter), is a far cry from the manicured Mondo tracks that miler Jeff Atkinson, nicknamed Rat, burned up in his heyday. Nevertheless, the long-time peninsulan names the Skyline as his favorite running course. But what do you expect from a guy whose nickname is Rat?

Rat is best-known as the winner of the 1988 U.S. Olympic Trials 1,500 meters, where he upset favorite Steve Scott with a fierce final lap. The 3:52 miler was an Olympic finalist two months later in Seoul and continued to race road and track miles for eight more years. In 1996, after a near miss at making the Olympic squad, Rat announced his retirement from track competition.

Rat is not the only 1988 Olympian who favors the trail. Marathoner Nancy Ditz, a Woodside resident who lives a short jog from the foot of Huddart and Wunderlich Parks, also haunts these trails.

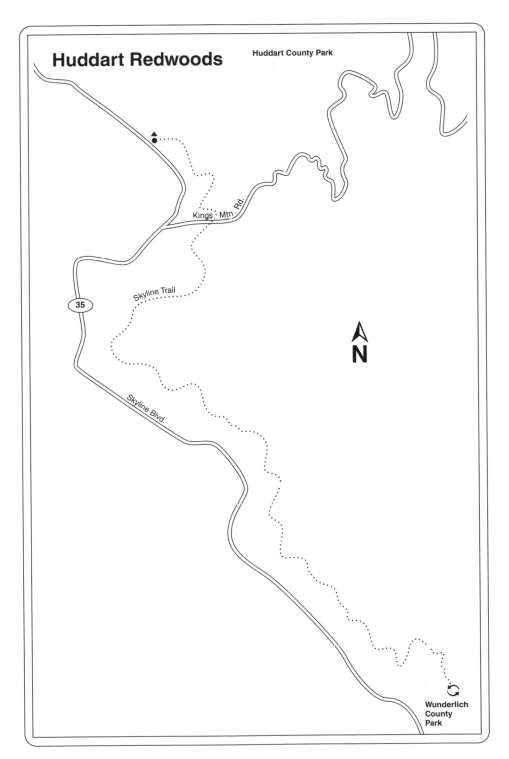

Huddart Redwoods

Huddart County Park

Kings · Mtn · Rd.

35

Skyline Trail

N

Skyline Blvd.

Wunderlich
County
Park

STANFORD HILLS

7.1 MILES	ROAD/TRAIL	SCENERY RATING				
	C	HILL RATING				

Track stars like PattiSue Plumer, Regina Jacobs, and Jeff Atkinson took their first steps toward Olympic glory on "the Farm," as Stanford University is fondly called by students and alumni. This route is a sampler of their training routes: an idyllic amalgam of rolling hills, quiet bike paths, and country roads southwest of campus that makes distance running a treat.

ACCESS

From San Francisco or San Jose, I-280 to Page Mill Rd. exit (Palo Alto). Park immediately west of the freeway at the Park & Ride lot at Arastradero Rd. The CalTrain-Stanford Stadium station is a 1-mile jog through campus to the route's 4-mile mark.

COURSE

Turn (R) from the lot onto Arastradero Rd. Just after passing under I-280, turn (L) onto the unmarked bike path (.7 mile) that parallels Arastradero Rd. At the Arastradero Rd.–Foothill Expwy. stoplight, cross Arastradero and after 20 meters turn (L) onto another unmarked bike path (1.9 miles), which passes Bol Park. Where the path ends at Hanover St. (3.2 miles), turn (R). At the end of Hanover St., jog (R) and then (L) onto Escondido, (L) on Campus Dr. (4.0 miles), first (L) on Bowdoin St., (R) on the bike path that parallels Stanford Ave. to its end at Junipero Serra Blvd. (5.3 miles). Cross at the light, turn (L) on the dirt shoulder, (R) on Page Mill Rd., and (R) on Old Page Mill Rd. (5.8 miles), which merges with Page Mill shortly before you complete the loop.

FOOT NOTES

The bad news is that you have to cross at three stoplights, endure a mile of busy streets (Junipero Serra Blvd. and Page Mill Rd.), and dash across two freeway ramps. The good news is that the rest of the run is exceedingly pleasant

Nearly half of the distance is on bike paths through wooded areas, past grazing horses, over footbridges, and alongside streams. The only real climb of the route lasts for a mile on a charming rural road (Old Page Mill). Most of the remainder of the route is a spin through the southwestern corner of the Stanford campus.

To add distance you may want to explore the campus, although the maze of dead-end streets and walking paths make it as complex as a graduate course in nuclear physics. For a jogging tour of landmarks like Stanford Stadium, Hoover Tower, and the Main Quad, turn (R) on Campus Dr. (the 4-mile mark) and find your way by reading signs and asking students. Another way to add mileage is to follow the very hilly trails on Stanford land that head west from the intersection of Stanford Ave. and Junipero Serra Blvd.

FARTLEK ON THE FARM

There is no richer soil for running than on "the Farm." Stanford cranks out Nobel winners and race winners alike; Stanford's men's and women's cross-country teams scored a rare sweep at the 1996 NCAA Cross-Country Championships. But what happens when the support network of coaches and teammates vanishes?

Jeff Johnson addressed this problem in 1995 by creating the Farm Team, a Nike-sponsored group of about 25 regional- and national-class distance runners. They train together at Stanford Stadium and run a modified version of this route on many of their distance runs. Johnson, a Stanford alumnus and the first full-time employee of Nike, is their volunteer coach. Nike covers shoes and most race travel expenses.

Says Johnson, "It's difficult for the postgraduate athlete to carry on. The Reebok Enclave [of world-class runners in Washington, DC] is a jewel, but there was nothing like that on the West Coast." Now there is.

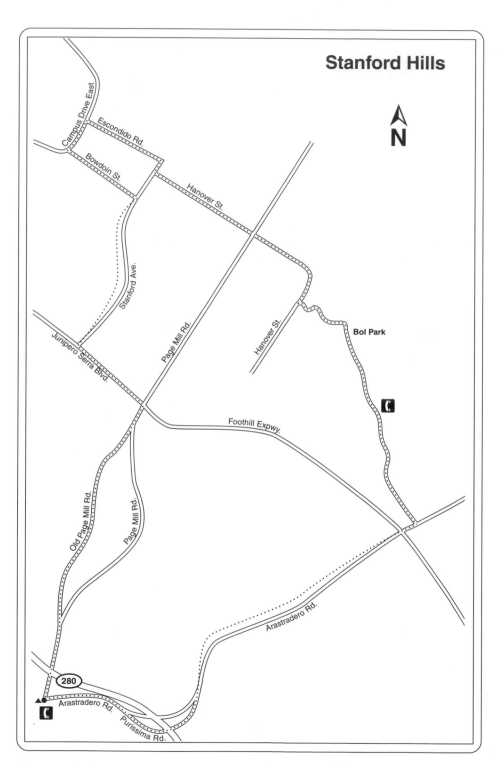

Stanford Hills

N

Campus Drive East
Escondido Rd.
Bowdoin St.
Hanover St.
Stanford Ave.
Page Mill Rd.
Junipero Serra Blvd.
Hanover St.
Bol Park
Foothill Expwy.
Old Page Mill Rd.
Page Mill Rd.
Arastradero Rd.
280
Arastradero Rd.
Purissima Rd.

RANCHO SAN ANTONIO

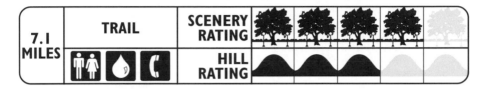

7.1 MILES	TRAIL	SCENERY RATING	HILL RATING

Why is this the most popular park for running in the Silicon Valley? How about miles of interconnecting, exceptionally well-marked and -maintained, evergreen-shaded trails—and a location two minutes off the freeway?

ACCESS

From San Francisco or San Jose, take I-280 to the Foothill Expwy. exit (Cupertino). Go south to the first (R) onto Cristo Rey Dr.; proceed 1.0 mile to the park entrance and .3 mile to the last parking lot. Or SCVTA bus #23 from downtown San Jose to Foothill/Cristo Rey.

COURSE

Main Route. From the lot, cross the wooden footbridge and turn (R) on the wide dirt path. At .3 mile, turn (L) at Open Space Preserve sign and take any of the trails, which are all gradually uphill, to Deer Hollow Farm. Just past the farm, turn (L) on Wildcat Canyon Trail (1.2 miles), angle (L) on Upper Wildcat Canyon Trail to its end (1.7 miles); then turn (R) on Upper High Meadow Trail (3.0 miles), (L) at the wide connecting trail to Rogue Valley Trail (3.3 miles), (R) on Rogue Valley Trail (4.3 miles) to the farm (5.9 miles), and retrace your steps to the parking lot.

Alternate Route (5.6 miles). For an easy out-and-back, on your first pass of the farm, take Rogue Valley Trail (instead of Wildcat Canyon Trail) until it reaches a steep uphill; then head back.

FOOT NOTES

Rancho is so runner-friendly that there are changing benches in the restrooms, and stretching bars and free trail maps at the entrance to the 23-mile web of trails. This route begins in a grassy meadow alongside an oak-shaded creek. As you start up narrow and gradually steepening

Wildcat and Upper Wildcat Trails, you cross bridges in a deeply shaded forest that calls to mind the coastal slopes of Mt. Tam.

At the 1,000-foot crest of Upper Wildcat, you're rewarded with a killer view—and soon confront a killer descent. Take it slowly! The last 2.8 miles (the alternate route's return trip) is a gorgeous, gentle descent on wide dirt paths between creeks, trees, and meadows.

The gates are open daily from 8:30 A.M. to 5:00 P.M. For information, call Mid-Peninsula Regional Open Space District, 408-691-1200.

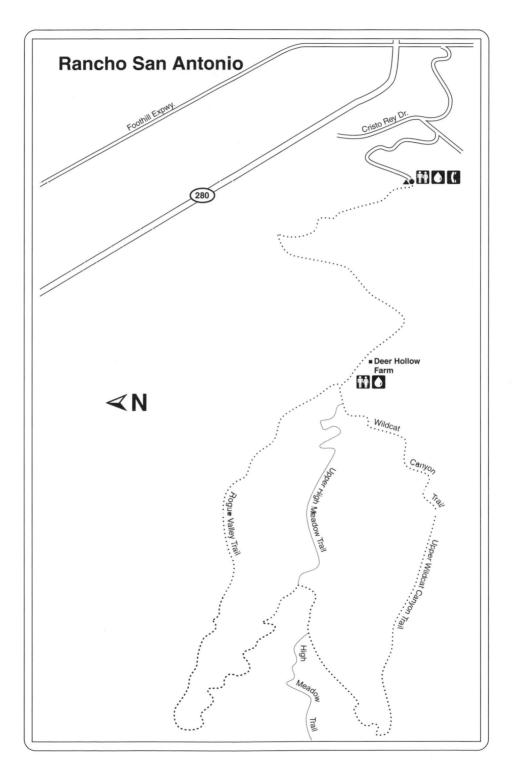

Rancho San Antonio

Foothill Expwy.

Cristo Rey Dr.

280

≺N

■ Deer Hollow
Farm

Wildcat

Canyon

Trail

Rogue Valley Trail

Upper High Meadow Trail

Upper Wildcat Canyon Trail

High

Meadow

Trail

LOS GATOS CREEK

6.4 MILES	ROAD/TRAIL	SCENERY RATING	
	👫 💧 (	HILL RATING	

Here's a slice of nature in the center of the suburban sprawl southwest of San Jose. Padding along a creek under oaks, sycamores, and willows, it's easy to forget that you are within .5 mile of teeming Hwy. 17 the entire way.

ACCESS

From San Francisco or San Jose, I-280 to Hwy. 17-South, Lark Ave. exit (Los Gatos). Turn (L) on Lark Ave. for .3 mile to (R) Los Gatos Blvd. After 1.0 mile, turn (R) on Blossom Hill Rd. and proceed .8 mile (just past Vasona Lake Park entrance); turn (R) on University Ave. and park immediately on right. Or CalTrain to Santa Clara, SCVTA bus #60 to the start.

COURSE

Walk down the path and stairs from the Blossom Hill Rd.-University Ave. intersection to a dirt path. Follow the path to the left, cross the pedestrian bridge at the carousel, then turn (L) on Los Gatos Creek Trail. Follow this bike path as it meanders along Vasona Lake, past (but not over) a dam, along Los Gatos Creek, over the creek on a pedestrian bridge (1.7 miles), and then downstream to the last of three fishing ponds at a big parking lot. Turn (L) and follow the dirt path (which soon becomes a dirt road) on the far shoreline of each pond. At the end of the last pond, the dirt road bears (L) back to the bike path. Turn (R) on the bike path and head back.

FOOT NOTES

The bike path is usually packed with runners, walkers, skaters, and cyclists. Alongside Vasona Lake, Los Gatos Creek, and then a trio of fishing ponds to the turnaround, you can choose between the bike path and an intermittent dirt shoulder. You can occasionally hear the hum of Hwy. 17, but the chatter of the mallards and geese often drowns it out. The entire route is in a waterfowl sanctuary.

To add distance, follow the bike path past the turnaround for up to 8 miles to San Jose. Or follow the bike path for up to 3 miles south from the finish to Lexington Reservoir. For info, call Vasona County Park, 408-356-2729.

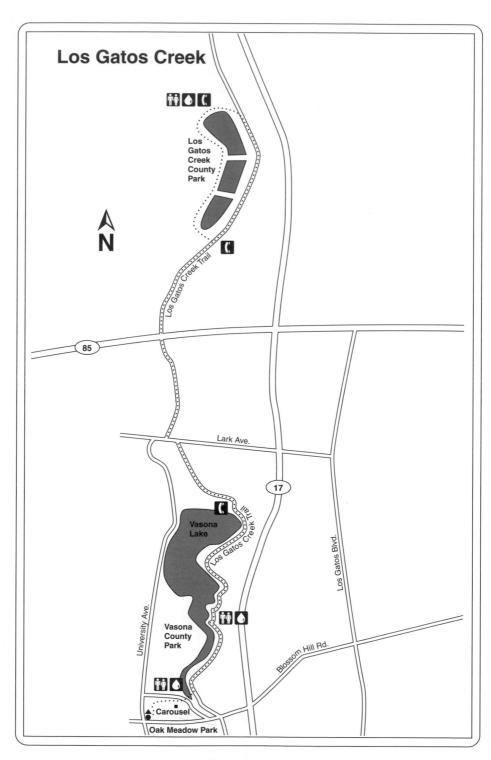

Los Gatos Creek

Los Gatos Creek County Park

Los Gatos Creek Trail

N

85

Lark Ave.

17

Vasona Lake

Los Gatos Creek Trail

University Ave.

Los Gatos Blvd.

Vasona County Park

Blossom Hill Rd.

Carousel

Oak Meadow Park

COYOTE CREEK PARK

11.7 MILES	ROAD	SCENERY RATING		HILL RATING

The Santa Clara Valley was crisscrossed by creeks before it was developed. This route, past tires hung from ropes over Coyote Creek by barefoot kids, recaptures the soothing sense of a quiet river valley—just a few miles from downtown San Jose. The illusion is shattered only briefly, during close encounters with Hwy. 101 and an office building.

ACCESS

From downtown San Jose, Hwy. 101-South to Coyote–Hellyer Park exit (south San Jose). Turn (L) on Hellyer Ave. (stop sign), and take an immediate (L) into the parking area; park on the right. There's a self-service parking fee of $3 on weekends and summer weekdays, although rangers say that only repeat offenders are ticketed. No public transit.

COURSE

Walk 50 meters to the creek bike path and start your run to the left. Follow the creek the entire distance. Signs direct you across the creek once (2.9 miles); be sure to make an immediate (L) off that bridge to stay along the creek. Turn back at Metcalf Park, a small city park with restrooms and a water fountain.

FOOT NOTES

Coyote Creek is not as scenic as the county parks in the hills west of San Jose, but it does have something they don't—level ground. Actually, it's gently undulating, with an occasional short pitch, but nothing to raise your pulse.

Except for the first mile, past barbecue areas and a trout pond, you'll encounter only a few runners, cyclists, and skaters. Little shade at midday, and gnats and mosquitoes in the evening are detriments.

Marathoners should know that the path continues south past the turnaround for another 9 miles. Park hours are 8:00 A.M. to dusk. For info and a map, call 408-225-0225 or 408-358-3741.

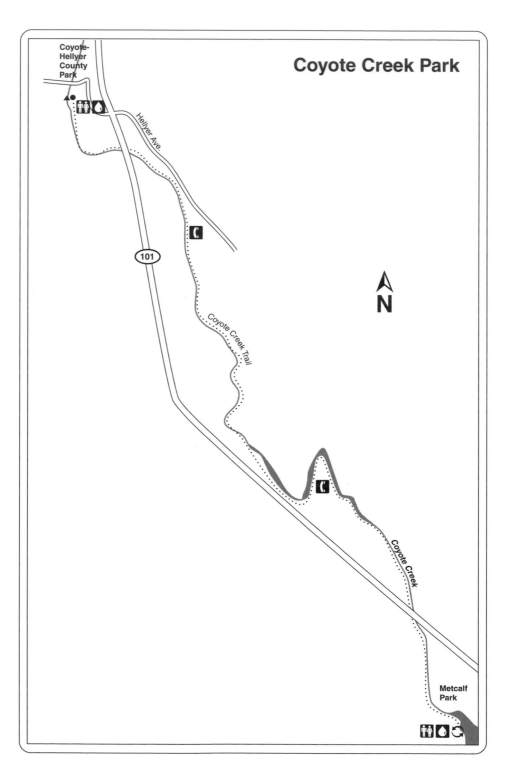

Coyote Creek Park

Coyote-Hellyer County Park

Hellyer Ave.

101

Coyote Creek Trail

N

Coyote Creek

Metcalf Park

SANBORN-SKYLINE PARK

| 8.2 MILES | TRAIL | SCENERY RATING | |
| | **(** | HILL RATING | |

Similarities to the Huddart Redwoods route described earlier in this chapter are uncanny. Although they are about 20 miles apart, both routes follow the Skyline Trail, both closely parallel Hwy. 35 on a ridge overlooking the ocean, and both run through the deep shade of evergreens on roller-coaster terrain. In short, both are great spots for trail runners to shake the city out of their bones.

ACCESS

From San Francisco or San Jose, I-280 to Hwy. 17-South. Take Bear Creek Rd. exit (at Lexington Reservoir), and go .4 mile; turn (L) on Black Rd. and travel 4.7 miles; turn (R) on Hwy. 35 (Skyline Blvd.) for 1.9 miles to an unmarked, six-car parking lot on the right, just beyond the "SCL 9.52" highway post. No public transit.

COURSE

The trailhead is on the north end of the lot. Follow Skyline Trail north, parallel to Hwy. 35, to Summit Rock Loop sign and turn (R). Keep left at all forks on this loop. At any time that you've had enough of the rigorous trails, you can switch to Hwy. 35 via any of the six obvious access points; then follow Hwy. 35 south to your car. This road alternative is not a bad one, as it offers gentle grades, few cars, and views to the ocean.

FOOT NOTES

The pretty, 15-minute drive from Hwy. 17 past Christmas tree farms should get you charged up for this run, which is the trail run closest to San Jose that you will find in the Santa Cruz Mountains. The course is wide and smooth in places, but mostly it's narrow and rough, with rocks, roots, and an occasional fallen tree keeping you on your toes. The weak of ankle should stay home. Add the constant hills, including switchbacks on the Summit Rock Loop, and you have a course that is both physically and mentally challenging.

Is it worth the effort? Nature is big and bodacious along this trail; there are massive trees (redwoods, firs, and oaks), and moss-covered boulders that attract novice rock climbers. Views of the ocean and the Santa Clara Valley, 2,800 elevation-feet below, add to the grandeur.

To add distance, you can drop into Sanborn–Skyline County Park on the Sanborn Trail (1.0 mile from the start), go farther north on the Skyline Trail toward Upper Stevens Creek County Park (4.5-mile mark), or cross Hwy. 35 at the Indian Rock trailhead to explore Castle Rock State Park's trails (5.5-mile mark). The latter trails connect through Big Basin all the way to the sea. All of these trails provide great training for hilly marathons like Big Sur. For info and a map, call 408-867-9959 or 408-358-3741.

THE OTHER BART

BART doesn't refer only to Bay Area Rapid Transit. The Bay Area Ridge Trail is the other BART, and another way to get around, albeit at a far less rapid pace. The Trail is an ambitious effort to ring the bay hills with trails. More than half of the planned 400-mile network is already in place, thanks to the efforts of employees and volunteers from dozens of nonprofit organizations and city and county parks.

Most of the trails trace the ridges above Bay Area cities, including Sanborn–Skyline Park's Skyline Trail. Among the other segments of the Bay Area Ridge Trail represented in this book are San Francisco's Fort Funston, Oakland's Redwood Park, the Marin Headlands, and Mt. Tam. To learn more, read *The Bay Area Ridge Trail* by Jean Rusmore (Wilderness Press 1995), or call the Bay Area Ridge Trail Council at 415-391-0697.

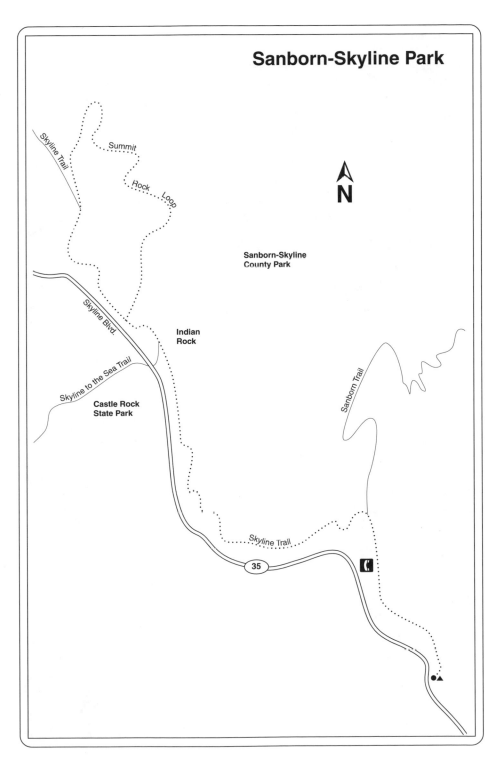

Sanborn-Skyline Park

Skyline Trail

Summit

Rock Loop

N

Sanborn-Skyline
County Park

Skyline Blvd.

Indian
Rock

Skyline to the Sea Trail

Sanborn Trail

Castle Rock
State Park

Skyline Trail

35

BAY AREA RACES

I look towards San Francisco and its surrounding cities and countryside as the nation's mecca for runners. Nowhere else do climate, geography, and running interest combine so well.

—*Joe Henderson, author of 20 running books*

Joe should know. When he lived in the Bay Area between 1967 and 1981 as a running writer and *Runner's World* editor, he was an avid Bay Area road racer. We shared many starting lines. Joe now lives in Oregon and writes a column for *RW*, but he still visits the Bay Area to run races like the Big Sur and Napa Valley Marathons.

In the early 1970s, there was a race every weekend in the Bay Area, which wasn't the case almost anywhere else. Today, only the number of races and runners has changed (growing tenfold).

Bay to Breakers is the biggest race in America, with about 75,000 participants. The Bay Area also hosts America's second-largest trail run (the Dipsea), three of the 30 largest marathons (Big Sur, San Francisco, and Napa Valley) and three of the 20 largest 10Ks (Wharf to Wharf, Mercury News, and Far Side). Those events and a few more, all of which I've run at least once, are featured in this chapter.

Bigger isn't always better, of course, but Bay Area races merge quantity with quality. Most are scenic, well-organized, and run on accurate courses, like those described in this chapter. The races cater to everyone, from elite runners who choose among dozens of prize-money races to fitness walkers who are welcome at almost every run. See the appendix for information on club runs, fun runs, and races besides these "top 10."

Use the contact information to request an entry form because most of these races do not accept race-day registration, and details can change from year to year. Also, organizers can apprise you of hotel discounts and race weekend activities.

Bay Area Races

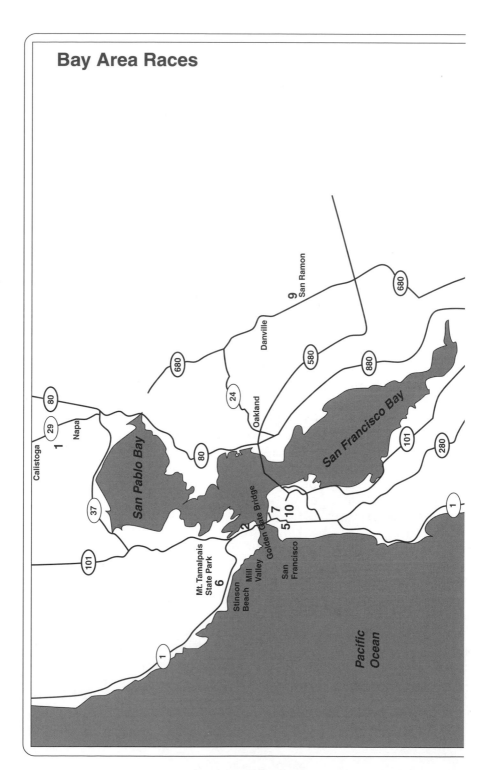

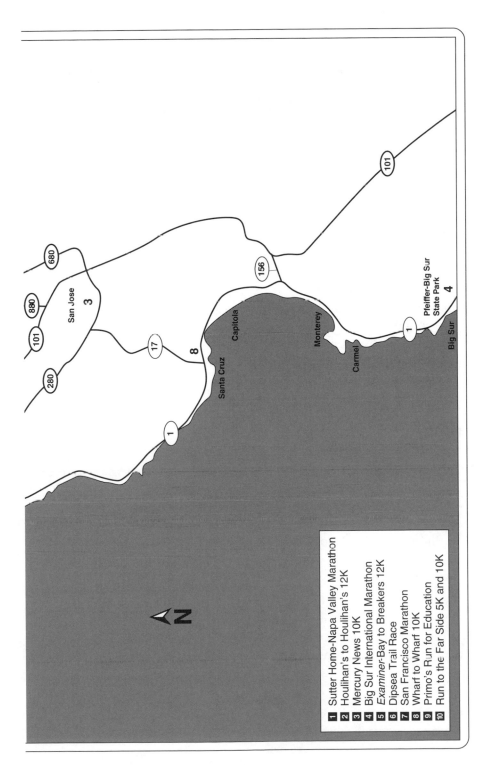

N

1 Sutter Home-Napa Valley Marathon
2 Houlihan's to Houlihan's 12K
3 Mercury News 10K
4 Big Sur International Marathon
5 *Examiner*-Bay to Breakers 12K
6 Dipsea Trail Race
7 San Francisco Marathon
8 Wharf to Wharf 10K
9 Primo's Run for Education
10 Run to the Far Side 5K and 10K

680

101
880
280

San Jose
3

17

280

1

Santa Cruz

8

Capitola

156

Monterey

Carmel

1

Pfeiffer-Big Sur
State Park

4

Big Sur

SUTTER HOME-NAPA VALLEY MARATHON

| 26.2 MILES | FIRST SUNDAY IN MARCH | SCENERY RATING | | | | | |
| | ROAD | HILL RATING | | | | | |

There's something to be said for moderation in choosing a marathon. At mega-marathons you end up fighting crowds not only at race functions, but more importantly, in the early miles of the race. At small marathons there is plenty of running room—sometimes too much in the lonely later miles—but crucial amenities such as accurate split times and a traffic-free course are often missing.

Napa Valley is comfortably moderate, with the perks and solid organization of the big marathons but without the subway-like over-crowding. The customary field of 1,500 is just right.

ACCESS

It is less than a one-hour drive (or Greyhound trip) from San Francisco or Oakland to the Napa Valley. Take I-80-East, Hwy. 37-West, Hwy. 29-North, and turn (R) at El Centro Ave. (second Napa stoplight). Go two blocks to Vintage High School (the finish line), where you can catch the shuttle bus to the start in Calistoga. There is limited parking in Calistoga lots, but no post-race shuttle.

COURSE

The race starts in Calistoga on the Silverado Trail (at Rosedale Ave.). The course follows the two-lane country road all the way to Napa. At 23 miles, turn (R) on Oak Knoll Ave., (L) on Big Ranch Rd., (R) on El Centro Ave. to Vintage High School.

FOOT NOTES

The Napa Valley is world-famous for its wines, but Bay Area visitors enjoy it as much for the colorful, endless acres of vineyards as for the end product of those pampered plants. During the marathon, the vineyards are usually ablaze in mustard blossoms, and flowering plum trees decorate the course. You can admire this understated splendor during the one-way shot down the entire length of the narrow valley. All but the last half mile of the route is rural.

The course features a net elevation drop of 285 feet, with three mild uphill and downhill grades in the first 7 miles, then very gradual rolling and flat areas the rest of the way. Hundreds of runners use the Napa Valley Marathon each year as a last-minute Boston qualifier; about one-third of each year's finishers run personal bests. Most of the route is closed to traffic.

On race day the weather could be a rainy 36 degrees or a sunny 60 degrees, but is usually somewhere in between with fog giving way to sunshine as you run. Aid stations, staffed by hundreds of volunteers, are generously placed every two miles. Pre-registration is required.

Contact SHNVM, Box 4307, Napa, CA 94558. Hotline 707-255-2609; http://www.napa-marathon.com/.

DESTINATION NAPA

Marathon weekend activities typically include a sports and fitness expo, celebrity guest speaker, and pasta feed. What makes this a great destination race, however, is what you can do in the days before and after race weekend in the Napa Valley.

Tours and tastings are offered daily at most of the valley's dozens of wineries. The region is also becoming recognized for its "California cuisine" restaurants, which emphasize fresh ingredients. Between eating and drinking, you have a choice among hot springs spas near Calistoga, champagne brunches, hot air balloon rides, bike rentals, and more.

Where to stay? Accommodations range from $800 suites to $20 campsites. For information and reservations, call the Napa Valley Visitors Bureau at 707-226-7459.

TIP

Traveling with a spouse or friend who hates waiting around? The Three R's 5K Run/Walk starts and finishes at the high school on marathon morning. For information, call 707-253-3686.

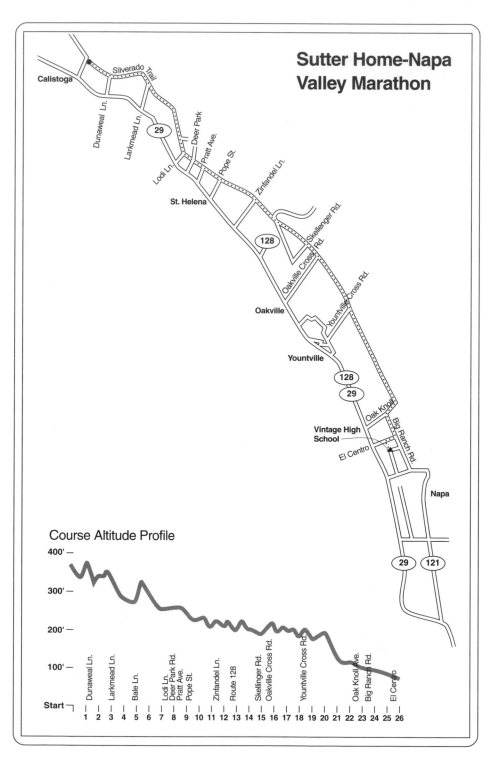

Sutter Home-Napa Valley Marathon

Calistoga
Silverado Trail
Dunaweal Ln.
Larkmead Ln.
Lodi Ln.
29
Deer Park
Pratt Ave.
Pope St.
Zinfandel Ln.
St. Helena
128
Skellenger Rd.
Oakville Cross Rd.
Yountville Cross Rd.
Oakville
Yountville
128
29
Oak Knoll
Big Ranch Rd.
Vintage High School
El Centro
Napa
29 121

Course Altitude Profile

400' —
300' —
200' —
100' —
Start ⌐

| Dunaweal Ln. | Larkmead Ln. | Bale Ln. | Lodi Ln. | Deer Park Rd. | Pratt Ave. | Pope St. | Zinfandel Ln. | Route 128 | Skellinger Rd. | Oakville Cross Rd. | Yountville Cross Rd. | Oak Knoll Ave. | Big Ranch Rd. | El Centro |

1 2 3 4 5 6 7 8 9 10 11 12 13 14 15 16 17 18 19 20 21 22 23 24 25 26

HOULIHAN'S TO HOULIHAN'S 12K

12K	FOURTH SUNDAY IN MARCH	SCENERY RATING	🌳	🌳	🌳	🌳	
	ROAD	HILL RATING	⛰	⛰	⛰		

There's an allure to crossing the Golden Gate Bridge by foot. When it was closed to traffic on its 50th birthday, there were so many pedestrians that the bridge visibly sagged. You won't need to wait for the 100th birthday, or train for the San Francisco Marathon, to be part of a bridge-crossing throng. The Houlihan's to Houlihan's water-hugging course follows a breathtaking route in the Golden Gate National Recreation Area and Presidio National Park, and on the west sidewalk of the bridge.

ACCESS

Buses leave Aquatic Park (next to Fisherman's Wharf) and downtown Sausalito for the East Fort Baker start about an hour before race time. The race packet includes details; there is no race-day registration.

COURSE

From the start on East Rd. at East Fort Baker, turn (R) on Murray Circle, (R) on East Rd., up to the pedestrian ramp to the west sidewalk of the Golden Gate, across the bridge to the view area parking lot, (L) on Lincoln Blvd., (L) on Halleck St., (L) on Mason St., (L) on Bank St., (L) on Old Mason St., straight onto Marina Blvd., up the Fort Mason pedestrian path to the foot of Van Ness Ave., (R) on Van Ness, and (L) onto the pedestrian path through Aquatic Park to the finish.

FOOT NOTES

Just as there are euphemisms in real estate ads—cozy means cramped, classic means crumbling—so there are on entry forms. In the Bay Area, any time a flier uses the word "scenic," it's code for "hilly." The flier for Houlihan's calls it "one of the most magnificent running courses anywhere in the world." That means really hilly. But it is magnificent.

There are only two hills, but the first one's a killer. In the second mile is a half mile of switchbacks from the water's edge to the bridge. The climb continues gradually for another half mile to the crest in the middle of the bridge, followed by a gradual downhill on the bridge, then a steep downhill to the bay waters. The second half of the course, if your legs have anything left, is flat except for a good-sized climb and descent at Fort Mason in the last mile.

With the field ranging from 4,000 to 5,000 in recent years, positioning at the front is an issue, especially because of the narrow road and bridge sidewalk in the first 2 miles. Organizers address the problem with a three-wave start, assigned by previous 10K or 12K time. The swiftest are sent off first and the other two waves follow at five-minute intervals.

The course is truly spectacular, taking in the rural beauty of now-defunct East Fort Baker, the majesty of the Golden Gate bridge, the historic buildings of the Presidio, and the urban beauty of the Marina district. To cap it off, the Aquatic Park lawn is a delightful spot to rest your bones at the finish, and there are parties at both Houlihan's.

Contact RhodyCo Productions, 1417 Irving St., San Francisco, CA 94122. Hotline 415-564-0532; runrhody@aol.com.

WHO'S HOULIHAN?

There isn't a Houlihan's in sight at the start or finish, but the old course connected the popular restaurants in Sausalito and San Francisco. As to how the race got started, that's a long story—635 miles long.

Dave Rhody was a waiter at Houlihan's in San Francisco in 1982 when he asked the chain to sponsor him on a run connecting all seven Houlihan's restaurants from Newport Beach to Sausalito. The fund-raising run for Special Olympics took him 19 days. One year later, he went into the race-directing business by putting on the first Houlihan's to Houlihan's, with Joe Montana as celebrity host. Rhody and his company, RhodyCo, now put on several major Bay Area runs, including the Run to the Far Side.

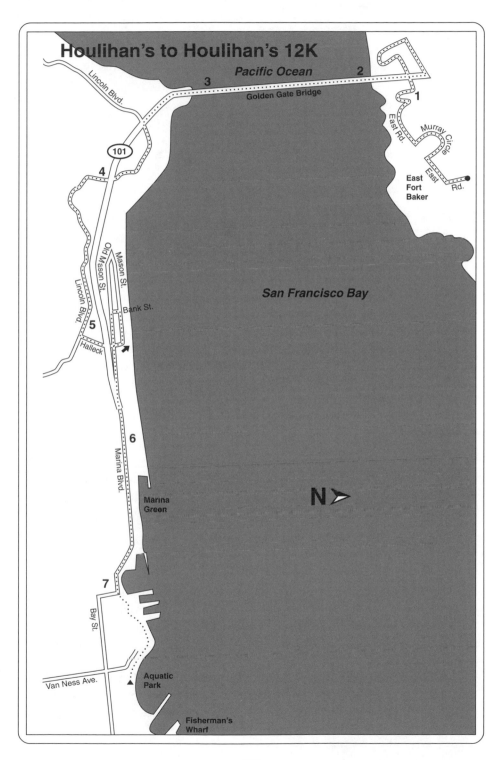

Houlihan's to Houlihan's 12K

Pacific Ocean

San Francisco Bay

Golden Gate Bridge

Lincoln Blvd.

101

Old Mason St.

Mason St.

Bank St.

Lincoln Blvd.

Halleck

Marina Blvd.

Marina Green

Bay St.

Van Ness Ave.

Aquatic Park

Fisherman's Wharf

East Rd.

Murray Circle

East Fort Baker

East Rd.

N

MERCURY NEWS 10K

10K	A SUNDAY IN MARCH	SCENERY RATING					
	ROAD	HILL RATING					

Like so many Bay Area runners, my 10K personal best was run at the "Merc." For more than 20 years, this has been the place to run fast, thanks to a pancake course and weather that's usually ideal for running.

ACCESS

Take I-280 to Hwy. 87-North (San Jose), Santa Clara St. exit. Find street parking a few blocks from the start and finish at Park–Almaden Ave. intersection. SCVTA light-rail is free by showing the driver your bib number; get off at the Convention Center station, two blocks from the start.

COURSE

From Park–Almaden Ave. intersection, run north on Almaden, (L) on Santa Clara, (L) on Autumn, (R) on Park Ave., (L) on McDaniel, (L) on Dana, (R) on Naglee, (R) on Garden, (R) on University, (R) on The Alameda/Santa Clara, (R) on Market, (R) on Park Ave. to the finish.

FOOT NOTES

San Jose may have overtaken San Francisco in population a few years ago, but it's no San Francisco. It lacks the waterfront and the million-dollar views, and the high-rises aren't that high. Downtown San Jose has been revitalized, however, with new hotels, restaurants, and office buildings, and it comes alive when 10,000 runners and walkers take it over on race day.

You'll run past the San Jose Arena (home of the NHL's Sharks) in the first mile and Rose Garden Park in the third mile, but most of the course is residential or commercial. Only in the first and last quarter mile do you see spectators and semi-high-rises.

Enough negativity. The course is flat and fast, and after finishing you can wander over to the Spring Festival in Guadalupe River Park with the other runners and 5K walk finishers.

Contact SJMN Race, 750 Ridder Park Dr., San Jose, CA 95190. Hotline 408-920-5755; http://www.sjmercury.com/10k/.

TIP

To run unimpeded, arrive early to secure a spot near the front. If you're fast enough, however, your spot will be guaranteed. Entrants who meet the elite standards—from 33:30 for open men to 42:30 for masters women in a 10K run during the previous year—are ushered into the seeded area at the front of the pack.

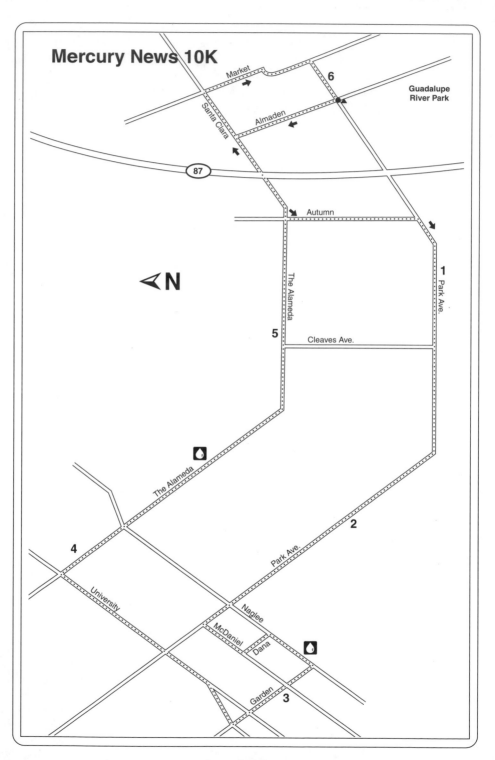

Mercury News 10K

BIG SUR
INTERNATIONAL MARATHON

26.2 MILES	LAST SUNDAY IN APRIL	SCENERY RATING	🏖️ 🏖️ 🏖️ 🏖️ 🏖️
	ROAD	HILL RATING	⛰️⛰️⛰️⛰️

There is no prettier course in America and runners from first to last are pampered as if the marathon is run for their sake alone. Is there anything else you want from a marathon? A fast course? Forget it. Unless this is your first marathon, as it is for many Big Sur-vivors each year, don't expect a personal best. Do expect to "hurt so good" after following the Pacific Coast Highway from Big Sur to Carmel in southern Monterey County's rugged coastal uplands.

ACCESS

From San Francisco or San Jose, Hwy. 101-South, Hwy. 156-West, Hwy. 1-South to Rio Road at Carmel's Crossroads Shopping Center (finish line), (L) on Carmel Valley Rd., proceed to Carmel Middle School for shuttle buses to the start at Pfeiffer Big Sur State Park. Greyhound stops in Monterey.

COURSE

Hwy. 1-North all the way from Big Sur to Carmel.

FOOT NOTES

Since its inaugural year in 1986, Big Sur has captivated the hearts and soles of runners across the nation. It's also broken a few. Succumb to the temptation of running too fast over the gradually descending first 9.6 miles (to Little Sur River Bridge) and you will simply *succumb* later on.

The 2.3-mile, 460-elevation-foot rise from the Little Sur River Bridge to Hurricane Point is the most dramatic hill, but it's early enough that patience and a short stride will not cause you much anguish. That will come soon enough, in the relentlessly rolling (though never steep) second half. You will know when you reach halfway, too. That's where you cross breathtaking Bixby Bridge, perhaps the most photographed single-span concrete arch bridge in the world.

While spectacular bridges and cliffs decorate the middle of the course, the first and last quarters have their own appeal: rolling pastures, quiet beaches, and groves of cypress and redwoods.

There are companion events for the marathoners' friends and families. Starting and finishing at the marathon finish line is a gorgeous 5K run/walk combining hills and wide dirt paths that are within stone-throwing distance of the surf. Walkers have three other options: a 7- or 10-miler in the extraordinarily scenic middle of the course or a 21-mile power walk that covers the last four-fifths of the course. The 1,500 walkers in 1997 mixed with the marathon's crowd of 3,200. The five-person marathon relay is yet another option. Pre-registration is required for all events except the 5K.

The marathon is a great excuse to vacation on the Monterey peninsula. The wildflowers are ablaze in April and you can visit the beaches, hike at Point Lobos State Reserve, golf at Pebble Beach, jog from Cannery Row to Lovers Point, or shop in world-famous Monterey or Carmel.

Contact BSIM, Box 222620, Carmel, CA 93922-2620; 408-625-6226; http://www.bsim.org/.

SIR SUR SPEAKS

Nobody has tamed the hills of Hwy. 1 like Brad Hawthorne. The Danville resident ran a never-approached-since 2:16:38 in 1987, two weeks after he was the top American finisher at the Seoul World Cup Marathon. He went on to record five more Big Sur wins (1989 to 1993) and now competes as one of America's leading runners over age 40.

"It's unusual for guys in the lead pack to look around at the scenery, but it happens at Big Sur," says Hawthorne. "Besides, it takes your mind off the pain!"

How do you handle those hungry hills? "Like any marathon," says Brad, "the key is to run an even effort. That means not pushing it too hard up the climbs—take them one step at a time—or trashing your thighs by going out of control on the descents."

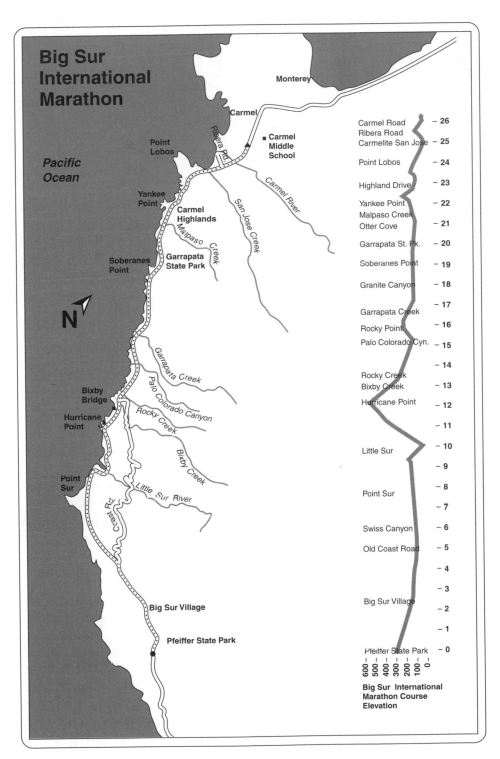

Big Sur
International
Marathon

Monterey

Carmel

■ Carmel
Middle
School

Pacific
Ocean

Point
Lobos

Ribera Rd.

Carmel River

Yankee
Point

Carmel
Highlands

San Jose Creek

Malpaso Creek

Soberanes
Point

Garrapata
State Park

N

Garrapata Creek

Palo Colorado Canyon

Bixby
Bridge

Rocky Creek

Hurricane
Point

Bixby Creek

Point
Sur

Coast Rd.

Little Sur River

Big Sur Village

Pfeiffer State Park

Carmel Road — 26
Ribera Road
Carmelite San Jose — 25

Point Lobos — 24

Highland Drive — 23

Yankee Point — 22
Malpaso Creek
Otter Cove — 21

Garrapata St. Pk. — 20

Soberanes Point — 19

Granite Canyon — 18

— 17

Garrapata Creek

Rocky Point — 16
Palo Colorado Cyn. — 15

— 14

Rocky Creek
Bixby Creek — 13

Hurricane Point — 12

— 11

Little Sur — 10

— 9

Point Sur — 8

— 7

Swiss Canyon — 6

Old Coast Road — 5

— 4

— 3

Big Sur Village — 2

— 1

Pfeiffer State Park — 0

600 — 500 — 400 — 300 — 200 — 100 — 0 —

**Big Sur International
Marathon Course
Elevation**

EXAMINER-BAY TO BREAKERS 12K

12K	THIRD SUNDAY IN MAY	SCENERY RATING					
	ROAD	HILL RATING					

Bay to Breakers is a race of superlatives. It's the biggest race in America, with 50,000 to 100,000 runners each year since 1982, and the oldest in the West, dating back to 1912. It's also the zaniest sporting event on the planet, with thousands of costumed crazies running amok and a few crazies running in nothing at all.

ACCESS

From downtown San Francisco hotels it's a short walk to the start at Howard St. and Spear St., but otherwise, public transportation is your best bet. From elsewhere in San Francisco, catch a MUNI bus or trolley (415-673-MUNI). From the East Bay, hop a BART train (510-465-BART). From the South Bay, take CalTrain (800-660-4287) or a SamTrans bus (800-660-4287). From the North Bay, ride a ferry (415-455-2000). In each case, "Breakers special" departures are added; details are provided in the race packet (race pre-registration is required).

If you must drive, expect to park a mile or two from the start or finish. Allow ample time for the cramped, pre- or post-race MUNI bus or trolley ride made necessary by the point-to-point course.

COURSE

The race starts with two essentially flat miles up Howard St., (R) onto 9th St., and (L) onto Hayes St., but the hordes will slow your pace. Just when you're able to swing your elbows and stride out, you will stride up six lung-searing blocks to the top of the Hayes St. hill. This is the only climb on the course. Over the top is a two-block descent on Hayes, then turn (L) on Divisadero for a block (the 3.0-mile mark), then (R) on Fell St. for 10 blocks alongside the Golden Gate Park panhandle. After entering the Park (4.0 miles), the course is flat and then downhill on Kennedy Dr. to the breakers. A (L) on the Great Hwy. puts you within sight of the finish line.

FOOT NOTES

The vast majority of Breakers runners don't race it, they experience it. The only way to avoid the gridlock that adds aggravating minutes to your finish time is to be fast enough for the seeded or sub-seeded sections, which requires a qualifying time such as a 10K under 35:00 for men or 42:00 for women. Either that or arrive before dawn and be prepared to defend your spot!

With transportation hassles and the Manhattan-like crowding, why bother? Because everyone should run Breakers once, and it seems that almost everyone in the Bay Area has. How else could the race keep replenishing its annual field of about 75,000, even with 25,000 nonreturning runners each year?

Bay to Breakers is a once-in-a-lifetime experience for all but the rabid. There is the thrill of the throng whooping and hollering all the way across the city; the agony of da feet after trudging up Hayes St. and pounding through the park; and the Woodstock-like Footstock, the post-race festival where Kenyans pocket checks and give speeches, costumed crazies disrobe, and everyone sticks around for the band. San Franciscans love a party and there is none any bigger. If running or walking 7.5 miles wasn't required, it would probably draw a million.

Contact Examiner-Bay to Breakers, Box 429200, San Francisco, CA 94142. Hotline 415-808-5000, ext. 2222; http://www.sfgate.com/breakers/.

BREAKERS BREAKDOWN

Smallest crowd (1963): 25

Largest crowd (1986): 102,000

Men's course record (Ismael Kirui, 1993): 33:42

Women's course record (Delillah Asiago, 1995): 38:23

Time elapsed before last runner crosses the *starting line:* 45:00

Course record by a "centipede" (Reebok Aggies, 1991): 37:40

Minimum number of linked runners required to qualify as a centipede: 13

Number of costumed runners in 1940: 1 (Captain Kidd)

Estimated number of costumed runners in 1997: 4,000

Pasta consumed at the pre-race party (in miles): 300

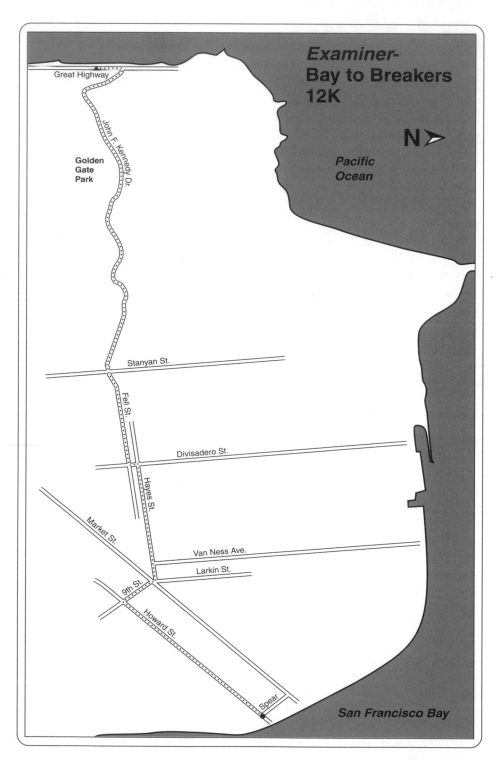

Examiner-
Bay to Breakers
12K

N

Pacific
Ocean

Great Highway

John F. Kennedy Dr.

**Golden
Gate
Park**

Stanyan St.

Fell St.

Divisadero St.

Hayes St.

Market St.

Van Ness Ave.

Larkin St.

9th St.

Howard St.

Spear

San Francisco Bay

DIPSEA TRAIL RACE

7.1 MILES	SECOND SUNDAY IN JUNE	SCENERY RATING	
	ROAD/TRAIL	HILL RATING	

If you were to rate Bay Area races for the intangible of character, the Dipsea would win with ease. Steeped in tradition and steep in the literal sense, it's the second-most popular trail race in America—and if the field wasn't limited to 1,500 runners, the race would outdraw the slightly larger Pikes Peak Ascent in Colorado. It's also the second-oldest major race in the United States, dating back to 1905. By the measurement of character, many runners would rank it second to only one race on the continent—the older and more prestigious Boston Marathon. It's that special.

ACCESS

From San Francisco, drive Hwy. 101-North to four miles north of the Golden Gate Bridge; exit onto Hwy. 1 (toward Stinson Beach). Turn (R) on Almonte Blvd., and (L) on Miller Ave. Park before you reach downtown Mill Valley, where there is a two-hour parking time limit. Jog up Miller Ave. to its end at Throckmorton Ave. (the start). There is no weekend bus service to the start.

COURSE

It would take several pages to describe the nuances of this course, with its mixture of stairs, fire roads, paved roads, and trails, including one trail that's open only on race day. Complicating matters is that it's an "open" course—sort of. Part of the appeal of the race is that you're allowed to get from Lytton Square in Mill Valley to Stinson Beach any way you wish, so runners take a variety of shortcuts. But some shortcuts have been pronounced illegal to protect vegetation and private property, so now there are legal and illegal shortcuts.

The bottom line: If you are lucky enough to get a race entry, go whichever way the folks ahead of you are going. If you are really motivated, train on May weekends on the easily-navigated later portions of the Dipsea Trail (from Muir Woods to the westernmost point of Panoramic Hwy.) and you will encounter Dipsea veterans. Ask to join them, and plead for advice. Good luck.

FOOT NOTES

This course is a monster. Within 600 meters of the start, you pant up the infamous Dipsea Steps, 676 stairs in three flights, with the only breathers at road crossings. Then the course goes up and up, down and down, and up and up again. Oh, there's a mile or two of rolling grasslands in the middle, but then it's down, down, down on ankle-twisting trails where the deep shade conceals treacherous roots. Nonetheless, expect to be intoxicated by the adventure and the beauty of the redwood-groved slopes of Mt. Tamalpais.

A unique wrinkle to this race is the age-handicapping. Runners are released in waves, with females, boys under age 19, and men over age 30 given head starts of one to 22 minutes. Truly, anyone can win. Request an entry by March (they're sent out April 1) and return it the same day it's received. That will usually get you in.

To learn more about this classic, read Barry Spitz's book, *Dipsea: The Greatest Race* (Portrero Meadow 1993, 415-454-2769).

Contact Dipsea Trail Race, Box 30, Mill Valley, CA 94942. Hotline 415-331-3550; http://www.dipsea.org/.

KING OF THE TRAIL

Sal Vasquez is the king. Combining his agility as a retired professional soccer player and his endurance as a record-setting masters road racer since 1980, he won the Dipsea seven times between 1982 and 1997, five more times than anyone in race history.

His strategy? "I mix running and walking on the steps so that I'm not tired at the top," he says. "Then I run as fast as I can down to Muir Woods. I take it easy up that hill, but then I push it the rest of the way." His fearless plunges down the late-race log stairs, which he skips three or four at a time, are the stuff of legend. "If you fall," he shrugs with an amiable grin, "you just pick yourself up."

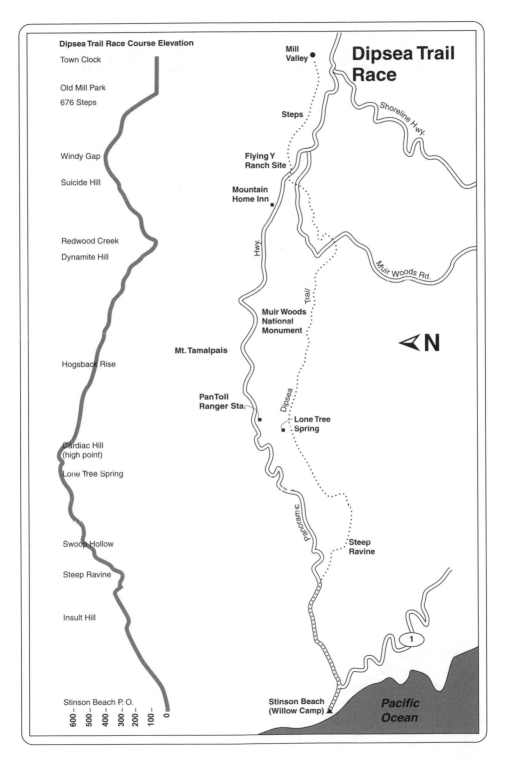

Dipsea Trail Race Course Elevation

Town Clock

Old Mill Park
676 Steps

Windy Gap

Suicide Hill

Redwood Creek
Dynamite Hill

Hogsback Rise

Cardiac Hill
(high point)

Lone Tree Spring

Swoop Hollow

Steep Ravine

Insult Hill

Stinson Beach P. O.

600 – 500 – 400 – 300 – 200 – 100 – 0

Dipsea Trail Race

Mill Valley

Shoreline Hwy.

Steps

Flying Y Ranch Site

Mountain Home Inn

Hwy.

Muir Woods Rd.

Trail

Muir Woods National Monument

Mt. Tamalpais

Dipsea

N

PanToll Ranger Sta.

Lone Tree Spring

Panoramic

Steep Ravine

1

Stinson Beach (Willow Camp)

Pacific Ocean

SAN FRANCISCO MARATHON

26.2 MILES	SECOND SUNDAY IN JULY	SCENERY RATING	
	ROAD	HILL RATING	

The route has changed repeatedly since the first San Francisco Marathon in 1977, but the race has always drawn a crowd. Organizers settled on the current course in 1993 and plan to stick with it. But the hills that make the city a favorite of tourists make it a test for runners. Many runners say that even the Big Sur Marathon, famous for its hills, is no tougher. So don't expect to run a great time, but do plan to *have* one.

ACCESS

Pre-registration is required and includes a ticket for an early-morning bus from Kezar Stadium (where you finish) or downtown San Francisco to the Golden Gate Bridge start.

COURSE

You don't need to scout the 48 turns on this circuitous tour of the city. The course is sufficiently crowded with runners on race day that you won't get lost, and sufficiently congested with auto and bus traffic on every other day of the year that a practice run is a crummy idea.

FOOT NOTES

The start on the traffic lanes of the Golden Gate Bridge is inspiring. The course then descends through the Presidio and makes a loop around the Palace of Fine Arts, followed by a tour of Yacht Harbor and Aquatic Park; a spin through the heart of North Beach, Chinatown, and the Financial District; and a bay-hugging romp along The Embarcadero, and south of Market St., to Potrero Hill.

The signs change to Spanish in the Mission district; then you reach Haight St. and climb the first major hill at the 14-mile mark. It's a rigorous grind, not as steep as the Bay to Breakers' Hayes St. hill, but longer. You get to relax for a few miles of flats and downhills through the Haight-Ashbury district, Golden Gate Park, and along the ocean, but then the tough have to get going. A swarm of climbs test your legs just where you don't need it—in the last 7 miles along Sunset Blvd. and through Golden Gate Park. The last mile to Kezar Stadium, where you finish with a lap on the track in front of thousands of spectators, is mercifully flat.

Joining the list of "destination" marathons that includes New York and Honolulu, San Francisco drew 70 percent of its runners from outside the Bay Area in 1997. Why? Because of the sights of the city, but also because it is one of the few major, cool-weather marathons you can find in the summer. On a typical race morning, fog smothers the bridge at the start and cool winds follow you around the course.

Contact SFM, Box 77148, San Francisco, CA 94107; 800-722-3466 (California only) or 916-983-4622.

PATIENCE PREVAILS

Here is 1996 winner Brad Lael's strategy for running the course: "Start out slow and relaxed on the early flats and downhills, then gradually pick up the pace. You might as well work the Haight Street hill, because it's followed by a lot of gradual descending. All the climbing in the closing miles is tough regardless of how you run the rest of it. It's a hard course, but the constantly changing surroundings make it go by faster."

TIP

If you like the idea of being part of a marathon, but can't put in the training, run the 5K held in conjunction with the San Francisco Marathon, and then cheer the marathoners across the finish. You won't have to rise as early, you can run a fast time on the flat course in Golden Gate Park (the start/finish is at Kezar Stadium), you can share in all the excitement, and you won't have to walk backwards on stairs for the next week! The five-person marathon relay is another option.

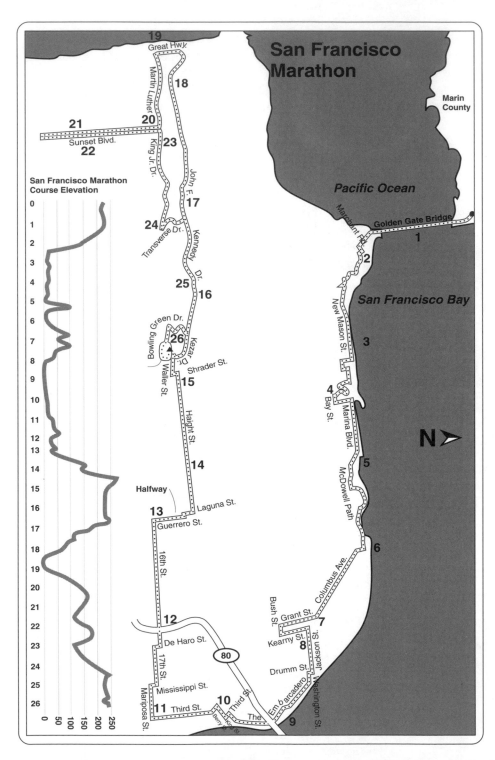

San Francisco Marathon

Great Hwy.

19

18

Marin County

Martin Luther

21   20

Sunset Blvd.

23

22

King Jr. Dr.

Pacific Ocean

John F.

Marguit Pl.

Golden Gate Bridge

1

17

2

24

Transverse Dr.

Kennedy

New Mason St.

San Francisco Bay

3

25   16

Dr.

Bowling Green Dr.

26

Kezar

Waller St.

Shrader St.

4

Bay St.

Marina Blvd.

15

Haight St.

N

McDowell Path

5

14

Halfway

13   Laguna St.

Guerrero St.

6

16th St.

Columbus Ave.

Bush St.

Grant St.

7

12

De Haro St.

Kearny St.

Jackson St.

80

8

17th St.

Drumm St.

Mississippi St.

Embarcadero

Washington St.

11   Third St.   10

Third St.

Mariposa St.

Berry St.

The

9

San Francisco Marathon Course Elevation

0
1
2
3
4
5
6
7
8
9
10
11
12
13
14
15
16
17
18
19
20
21
22
23
24
25
26

0   50   100   150   200   250

WHARF TO WHARF 10K

10K	FOURTH SUNDAY IN JULY	SCENERY RATING				
	ROAD	HILL RATING				

While organizers of most Bay Area races sweat over how to keep their races growing, Wharf to Wharf director Kirby Nicol turns runners away. For years, the race has "sold out" its 14,000 entry slots at least a month before the race. The lure is a festive event along the seaside, from the famous Santa Cruz Boardwalk to the Capitola Wharf.

ACCESS

From San Francisco or San Jose, drive I-280 to Hwy. 17-West. Continue on Hwy. 17 until it ends at Ocean St. in Santa Cruz. Look for race parking signs on Ocean St.

COURSE

From the start at the corner of Cliff St. and Beach St. at the Boardwalk, run east on Beach St., (L) on 3rd St., (R) on the Riverside Ave. bridge, (R) on San Lorenzo Blvd. to East Cliff Dr., (L) on Murray St., (R) on Lake Ave., (L) on East Cliff Dr., (L) on Opal Cliff/Cliff Dr. to the finish at Wharf Rd. in Capitola-by-the-Sea.

FOOT NOTES

Santa Cruz is packed with tourists every summer weekend, as it's been for generations, but on this late July weekend the restaurants fill with a different sort of tourist as the hot dogs-and-beer crowd is replaced by the PowerBars-and-Perrier crowd. Since 1972, many runners have made Wharf to Wharf an annual pilgrimage, turning it into a weekend for the whole family. Saturday at the Boardwalk and Sunday at the beach after the race is a nice double-header.

As for the race itself, the hills are nothing like the Boardwalk's Giant Dipper roller coaster—just plenty of gradual rollers, a 200-meter-long hill just past the one-mile mark and a swooping descent to the finish.

Entertaining you along the course are dozens of garage bands, with names like the Noisy Neighbors and the Dueling Julies.

Santa Cruz is the real draw; the race is simply an excuse to visit. There is something for everyone in this surfing, beachcombing, fishing, and university town.

Contact Wharf to Wharf, Box 307, Capitola, CA 95010. Hotline 408-475-2196; http://www.infopoint.com/orgs/wtwrace/.

THEY CAN'T STAY AWAY

Tom Wichelman and Bob Dunn smile when you ask them about the first Wharf to Wharf race in 1973. Neither had ever run a road race before that fateful day; neither had even run as far as six miles. But both finished the race and liked it well enough that they are among the handful who have run every one since.

The two met only recently, and discovered that they have more in common than the race. Both are Santa Cruz attorneys and both lavish praise on the race. Wichelman recalls that the first edition was decidedly low-key. "There were only 250 starters," he notes, "and now there are 50 times that many people. It's become a moving party. The crowding does mean that it's hard to run a fast time, but there are other races where you can do that. I run it every year with my wife and adult son. I consider it a celebration of good weather, good friends, and good health."

Dunn, now in his late 60s, adds, "The scenic course, the local flavor, and the race management are all excellent, and it's adapted real well to the growth of the field. I'll keep coming back as long as I can."

TIP

Arrive at least an hour early to allow time to park and walk to the start, and another half-hour to catch a post-race shuttle bus. If this bothers you, you don't have the right temperament to appreciate the beach-town ambiance anyway.

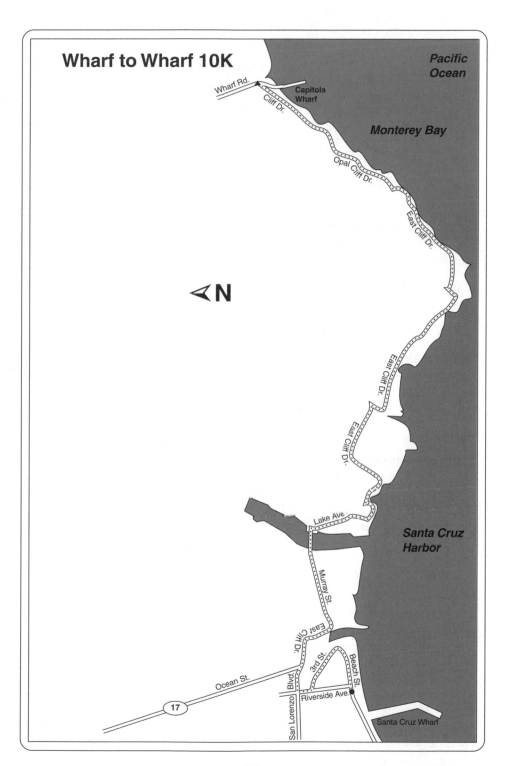

Wharf to Wharf 10K

Pacific
Ocean

Wharf Rd.

Capitola
Wharf

Cliff Dr.

Monterey Bay

Opal Cliff Dr.

East Cliff Dr.

◄N

East Cliff Dr.

East Cliff Dr.

Lake Ave.

Santa Cruz
Harbor

Murray St.

East Cliff Dr.

Ocean St.

San Lorenzo Blvd.

3rd St.

Beach St.

17

Riverside Ave.

Santa Cruz Wharf

PRIMO'S RUN FOR EDUCATION

5K, 10K, HALF MARA- THON	SECOND SUNDAY IN OCTOBER	SCENERY RATING					
	ROAD	HILL RATING					

If there's a charity that everyone agrees is worthy, it's the schools. Some of the Bay Area's fastest-growing road races are school fundraisers, led by this popular run in the San Ramon Valley.

ACCESS

5K and 10K. From Oakland, Hwy. 24-East, then I-680-South to the Bollinger Canyon exit (San Ramon), (L) .7 mile on Bollinger Canyon Rd. to San Ramon Community Center on the left. (From San Jose, I-680-North to Bollinger Canyon exit.) No public transit.

Half Marathon. Follow the 5K and 10K directions from Oakland to I-680-South but exit sooner at Diablo Rd. (Danville), (R) .5-mile on Diablo Rd. to Hartz Ave. (start), park anywhere. No public transit.

COURSE

There are numerous turns on the three courses, but you don't need to know the street names. The course is well-marked and well-populated.

5K. The course through downtown Danville is configured like a frying pan, with the start and finish at the end of the handle at the Marketplace shopping center.

10K. This course shares the first 2K with the 5K course, and then ventures farther into Danville. It's modern suburbia, start to finish.

Half Marathon. After leaving downtown Danville, you make 26 turns on roads and bike paths through suburban Danville and the sprawling business parks of San Ramon to the same finish line as the 5K and 10K.

FOOT NOTES

The 5K and 10K courses are essentially flat, and the half-marathon's gradual rises are few and far between. Timers will give you your split times at every mile. The starting line is crowded for the 5K only, which draws 2,500 of the event's 3,500 total starters.

Contact Primo's Run for Education, Box 1463, San Ramon, CA 94563. Hotline 510-279-6670.

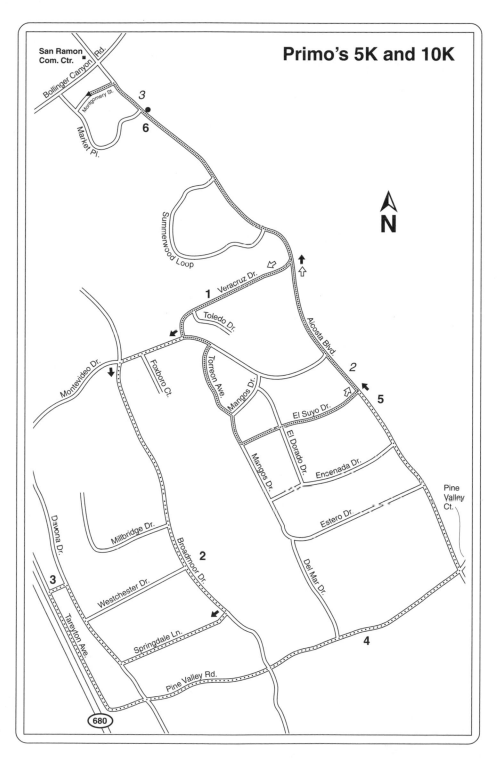

Primo's 5K and 10K

San Ramon
Com. Ctr.

Bollinger Canyon Rd.

Montgomery St.

Market Pl.

3

6

Summerwood Loop

N

Veracruz Dr.

1

Toledo Dr.

Alcosta Blvd.

Montevideo Dr.

Foxboro Ct.

Torreon Ave.

Mangos Dr.

2

El Suyo Dr.

5

El Dorado Dr.

Mangos Dr.

Encenada Dr.

Pine
Valley
Ct.

Davona Dr.

Millbridge Dr.

Broadmoor Dr.

Estero Dr.

Del Mar Dr.

2

Westchester Dr.

3

Tareyton Ave.

Springdale Ln.

4

Pine Valley Rd.

680

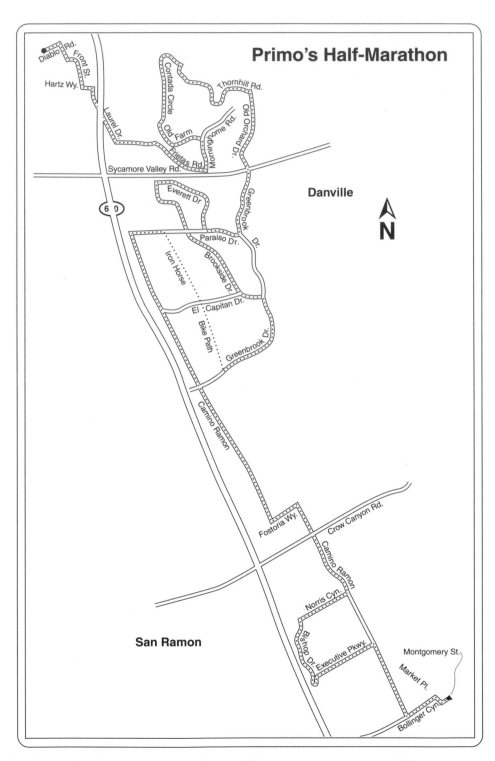

Primo's Half-Marathon

Danville

San Ramon

RUN TO THE FAR SIDE
5K AND 10K

5K, 10K	THANKSGIVING SUNDAY	SCENERY RATING	🌳 🌳 🌳				
	ROAD	HILL RATING					

Most of the runs staged in Golden Gate Park only draw a few hundred starters. So what's the reason for the success of the Run to the Far Side, which routinely attracts 10,000 to 14,000 participants? Is it the festive atmosphere and hilarious costume contest? Is it the proximity to Thanksgiving, which lets starters "run off" their feast? Or could it be the coveted T-shirt, drawn by cartoonist Gary Larsen? Probably all three.

ACCESS

Pre-registration is required; parking information is included in the race packet. (There are pay lots at nearby UCSF, USF, Kezar Stadium, and St. Mary's Hospital, and street parking on or near Fulton Street.) Or take the N-Judah trolley from downtown to 9th Ave. and walk to the start.

COURSE

5K. From John F. Kennedy Dr. and 8th Ave., go east on Kennedy Dr. and straight onto Oak St. at the Golden Gate Park panhandle. Turn (L) on Broderick St., (L) on Fell St., straight onto Kennedy Dr., and (L) on Concourse Dr. Sprint 100 meters to the finish.

10K. Start with the 5K runners and follow their course until shortly after re-entering Golden Gate Park. From Kennedy Dr., turn (R) on Conservatory Dr. for a loop behind the Conservatory of Flowers. Now turn (R) on Kennedy, (L) on Stow Lake, (L) on King Jr. Dr., (L) on Bowling Green Dr., (L) on Middle Dr., (R) on King Jr. Dr., (R) on Tea Garden Dr., and (R) on Concourse Dr. for 100 meters to the finish.

FOOT NOTES

Many consider this the fall version of Bay to Breakers, although the crowds are not so huge and the costumes are not quite so wild. It is San Francisco's second-largest run, but with fewer hassles. While Bay to Breakers draws runners from all over the world and grabs headlines, Far Side draws mostly locals and barely gets mentioned in the local papers.

Afterward, mingle with the finishers on the grand concourse between the De Young Museum and the California Academy of Sciences. Your well-earned T-shirt and other goodies are there and the band is rockin' on the Bandshell. There's even free childcare inside the Academy. Life is good.

The course? The 5K is close to pancake-flat, although the first half is ever-so-slightly uphill. The 10K lobs two hills at you: the Conservatory loop in the third mile and the Stow Lake incline one mile later, but neither is very long, and each is followed by a downhill.

Contact RhodyCo Productions, 1417 Irving Street, San Francisco, CA 94122. Hotline 415-564-0532; runrhody@aol.com.

T-SHIRT HYSTERIA

Nobody knows how many folks enter the Far Side run mainly for the T-shirt, but it isn't a small number. Says race director Dave Rhody, "We get a lot of calls from people who say, 'Can you sell us a shirt?' But we have to say no. Cartoonist Gary Larsen insists that the only way people can have a shirt is by entering the race. He wants the money and exposure for the Academy of Sciences."

Why is it so popular that the T-shirt has been reportedly resold for as much as $50? It seems there's a cult-like adoration for everything that Larsen creates, so the T-shirt, which displays a different Larsen-drawn illustration each year, is a hot commodity. As for the semi-retired Larsen, he has shown up at the race a few times but doesn't run much any more. He has told me it's due to injuries—something about a stampede of boneless chickens.

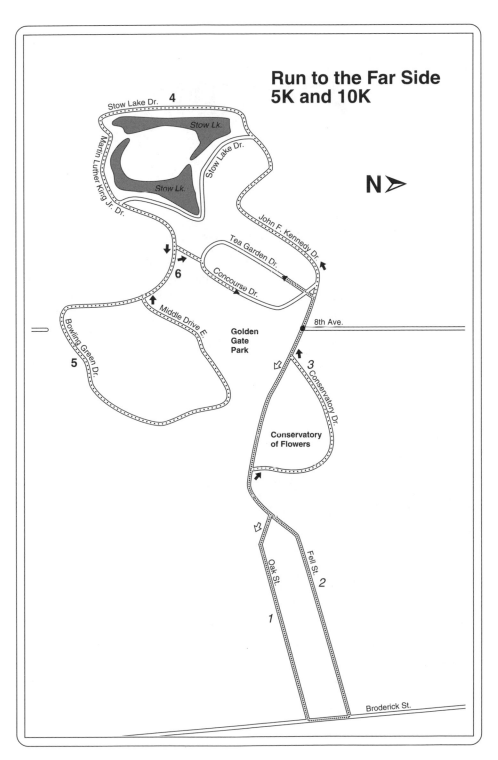

**Run to the Far Side
5K and 10K**

N

Stow Lake Dr.

4

Stow Lk.

Stow Lake Dr.

Martin Luther King Jr. Dr.

Stow Lk.

John F. Kennedy Dr.

6

Tea Garden Dr.

Concourse Dr.

Middle Drive E

Bowling Green Dr.

5

**Golden
Gate
Park**

8th Ave.

3

Conservatory Dr.

**Conservatory
of Flowers**

Oak St.

Fell St.

2

1

Broderick St.

APPENDIX

RUNNING CLUBS AND RACE ORGANIZERS

Listed here are Bay Area running clubs with ongoing group runs, where members and nonmembers alike are welcome. Write or call for details on the group runs or other club activities. Most of these clubs offer track interval workouts (usually on a Tuesday, Wednesday, or Thursday evening), host fun runs and social events, sponsor racing teams for competitive runners, and publish club newsletters.

Also included here is a list of Bay Area race circuits. There are hundreds of other Bay Area races and fun runs that are not part of these circuits. The most comprehensive race calendars are in *The Runner's Schedule* (415-472-7223 for subscription) and *Competitor* (free at bike shops and health clubs).

San Francisco

Dolphin South End Runners
Box 210482, San Francisco, CA 94121; 415-978-0837.
Tuesday evening, Wednesday evening, and Saturday morning runs from various city locations.

Frontrunners (gay and lesbian)
Box 300, San Francisco, CA 94114; 415-978-2429.
Tuesday evening runs at Ferry Building; Saturday morning runs at Stow Lake.

Pamakid Runners
Box 27557, San Francisco, CA 94127; 415-333-4780.

North Bay

Empire Runners
Box 5469, Santa Rosa, CA 95402; 707-544-2756.
Thursday evening runs at Howarth Park (Santa Rosa); Sunday
morning runs at various Sonoma County locations.

Tamalpa Runners Club
Box 701, Corte Madera, CA 94976, 415-892-0597
Weekly Sunday morning runs, Ross Common. Monthly Sunday
morning trail races at various locations.

East Bay

Diablo Road Runners
Box 31236, Walnut Creek, CA 94598; 510-906-8880.
Tuesday or Wednesday evening and Saturday morning runs at vari-
ous Walnut Creek and Danville locations.

East Bay Striders
4425 View Street, Oakland, CA 94611; 510-428-1200.
Sunday morning runs at various East Bay locations.

Forward Motion
412 Hartz Avenue, Danville, CA 94526; 510-820-9966.
Wednesday evening runs from store (412 Hartz Avenue).

Golden Bay Runners
Box 2144, Castro Valley, CA 94546; 510-484-1339 (evenings)
Tuesday evening and Sunday morning runs at Lake Chabot (San
Leandro).

Island City Runners
Box 1493, Alameda, CA 94501; 510-523-2647.
Monday and Thursday evening runs at Bay Farm Island (Alameda),
Lake Merritt (Oakland), and Redwood Park (Oakland).

Lake Merritt Joggers & Striders
12001 Broadway Terrace, Oakland, CA 94611; 510-601-7887.
Tuesday evening runs (April to October) at Redwood Park (Oakland). Monthly 5K, 10K, and 15K races at Lake Merritt (Oakland).

South Bay

Los Gatos Running Club
55 West Main Street, Los Gatos, CA 95030; 408-354-7365.
Early-morning runs daily from Los Gatos High School.

Palo Alto Run Club
759 Filip Road, Los Altos, CA 94024; 650-326-1250 and 650-964-8223.
Monday and Wednesday evening runs in Stanford and Palo Alto.

Stevens Creek Striders
Box 1176, Cupertino, CA 95015.
Saturday morning runs at Stevens Creek County Park (Cupertino);
Tuesday and Thursday evening runs (April to October) at Rancho
San Antonio Park (Los Altos).

West Valley Joggers & Striders
42210 Galleria Drive, San Jose, CA 95134; 408-435-2820.
Saturday morning runs from West Valley College (Saratoga).

RACE CIRCUITS

Three annual Northern California/Nevada Grand Prix prize-money
circuits are contested, including road races (distances ranging from one
mile to the marathon), ultramarathons (50K to 100 miles), and cross-
country races in the fall (5K to 10K). Pacific Assocation-USA Track &
Field, 120 Ponderosa Court, Folsom, CA 95630; 916-983-4622; http://
home.earthlink.net/~thomtrimble/PAUSATF.html.

About 10 large and festive runs and walks in the Bay Area are produced
annually by RhodyCo Productions, 1417 Irving Street, San Francisco,
CA 94122. Hotline 415-564-0532; e-mail runrhody@aol.com.

About 20 modest-sized run and walks scattered between San Francisco
and Aptos are conducted by The Final Result, 460 Wisnom Avenue, San
Mateo, CA 94401. Hotline 800-491-8988.

Weekly "fun races" are hosted by the DSE Runners (see the San
Francisco listing above for contact information) on Sundays at 9:30 A.M.
No hoopla, but what do you expect for a $3 entry fee?

ABOUT THE AUTHOR

Bob Cooper is a Bay Area native who started running in 1969. His first national magazine article was published in *Runner's World* four years later, and his articles on running and other fitness sports have been appearing ever since. Magazines that have published features by Bob include *American Health, Fitness, Forbes FYI, Condé Nast Sports for Women, Healthy Kids, Longevity, Men's Fitness, Men's Health, Men's Journal, Runner's World, Shape, Triathlete,* and *Women's Sports and Fitness.*

Bob was the executive editor of *Running Times* from 1990 to 1992 before he became a full-time freelance writer. He has published one previous book, *The Valley At Your Feet: 50 Walking, Running and Racing Courses in the Sacramento Valley.*

Bob's running achievements are also substantial. He is probably the only person to have participated in relay runs from the Pacific to the Atlantic (1973) and from Mexico to Canada (1983). His 50-mile time of 5 hours and 42 minutes ranked seventh in the United States in 1977, and he has run seven sub-2:30 marathons.

Top finishes include the Silver State Marathon (1st), Tucson Marathon (2nd), American River 50-Mile (2nd), San Francisco Marathon (3rd), and National 50-Mile Championships (4th). Since turning 40 in 1994, Bob has won numerous masters titles at Bay Area road races.

Bob lives in San Anselmo (Marin County) with his wife, Lisa, and two children, Brendan and Kira.

More Books for Runners

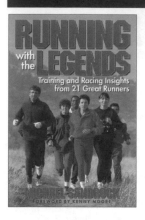

Michael Sandrock
*Foreword by
Kenny Moore*
1996 • Paper • 592 pp
Item PSAN0493
ISBN 0-87322-493-0
$19.95 ($29.95 Canadian)

"I feel I have 21 new friends in the running community. It's as if I've watched them compete and been right next to them through their triumphs and disappointments. When I have a question about my own running career, I can just open *Running With the Legends*, read a chapter, and my question will be answered."

Gwyn Coogan
10,000-meter Olympian, 1992
Twin Cities Marathon winner, 1995

David E. Martin, PhD,
and Peter N. Coe
*Forewords by
Sebastian Coe and
Anne Marie Lauck*
1997 • Paper
472 pp
Item PMAR0530
ISBN 0-88011-530-0
$22.95 ($33.95 Canadian)

"The first edition of *Better Training for Distance Runners* helped me make it to the 1996 Olympics and I believe this second edition can help me medal in the 2000 Olympics. The book allows runners to focus on specific events in distance running and explains the science of distance running in a manner that all distance runners can understand and use to their advantage."

Mark J. Coogan
U.S. Team Member
1996 Olympic Marathon

Tom Derderian
*Forewords by
Joan Benoit Samuelson
and Bill Rodgers*
1996 • Paper • 664 pp
Item PDER0479
ISBN 0-88011-479-7
$21.95 ($32.95 Canadian)

"I heard about the Boston Marathon as I was growing up in Kenya, and Tom's book gave me a better understanding of all those who have run before me. It makes my victories here even more special."

Cosmas Ndeti
Three-time Boston
Marathon Champion
Boston Marathon Men's
Record Holder, 2:07:15

Prices subject to change

HUMAN KINETICS
The Premier Publisher for Sports & Fitness
http://www.humankinetics.com/
2335

Place your order using the appropriate telephone number/address shown in the front of this book, or call TOLL-FREE in the U.S. 1-800-747-4457.